MAKING ARCHITECTURE

MAKING ARCHITECTURE

ANDREA DEPLAZES (ED.)

Professor Andrea Deplazes, Chair for Architecture and Technology at ETH Zurich
Projects from the First-Year Course

gta Verlag

Woodworks 1:1, Seminar week, Balaton, Hungary, 2003

Making Architecture

Andrea Deplazes

Architecture, like language, is a system. Rather than in words and sounds, it is expressed in physical elements: walls, partitions, ceilings, columns, supports, balconies, etc., and their omission, the opening. The earlier term, architectonic, clarifies the fact that it is not primarily the elements, per se, that are at issue, but instead, their assembling, connection, and composition (tectonic, which is the root of the word, is from ancient Greek and means framework of wooden beams). We also name this joining of elements a construction; this word indicates the (engineer-)technical material construction, the construct. Architectonic includes not only the construction, but also its relation to the architectural space whose creation and development is its actual purpose. One could, therefore, claim that for all engineers, the physical construct is the goal as he or she is a physicist specialized in mechanics and statics. The architect, however, concentrates on the architectonic space, which he or she is paradoxically only able to create via a detour through the physical construct; this is why architects inevitably become metaphysicists.

Architecture achieves significance only in connection with people. It is the designed environment that exists complementary to the natural (untouched) environment and assures survival in the world. Its scope extends from territorially defined areas determined by their urbanism through to very small, materially shaped aggregates distinguished by their detail. Beginning one scale lower are the material qualities and one higher, the geography. Thus, at issue are those dimensions that people can access directly; those that they can shape relevantly, and which, by means of feedback, directly influence them in their development. Architecture takes place everywhere, on a daily basis, regardless of whether we are consciously aware of it.

Accordingly, architecture deals with ideas about life, with designs and projections of life. It can model the three-dimensional scenarios necessary for doing so in the form of concepts, designs, visualizations, plans, diagrams, and models – primarily, graphic representations. These are open to discussion. Quite frequently, it is also the not-built architecture, "castles in the air", that move the world.

In the end, however, architecture only exists when it has become physical, when a social program has become an architectural project, and from that, in turn, a material and spatial object. At issue here is the transfer of a thought, a concept, into built architecture. At this moment, everything depends on whether this transfer occurs plausibly, meaningfully, and completely. That precisely is the issue when architecture becomes physical creation.

On the Use of Useless Things

Christoph Wieser

Suddenly, all I see are gloves. I imagine all of these objects, the fragile, delicate ones and the corporeal, heavy ones, as gloves. A bold idea, for sure. After all, barely a one is suitable for this purpose. Even when the caption indubitably identifies the structure as a glove, in many cases how to use the thing remains unclear. Nevertheless, the images continually lead me to move my fingers, in spirit, to make my hand small and lithe or long and claw-like, in the hopes of finding a way to "grasp" the construct on the photo by hand, to appropriate it in this way. Why do I desperately try to give these objects a meaning, or more precisely, a function, and thereby a clearly defined use? Why do I find it hard to see them for what they primarily are: finger exercises to train the ability to think architecturally? On the one hand, I catch myself taking the one picture with a hand as representative for all of the others without hands and imagine these, too, with hands. Similar to the way that the sitting person miraculously disappearing in the darkness of the Styrofoam block allows related objects to become chairs in my mind (including some that are quite comfortable, or so I imagine). On the other hand, without exception, the objects radiate seriousness, an intensity of occupation with materials, techniques for connecting and folding, possibilities of pouring, tying and pressing, which prohibit carelessly dismissing them as useless playthings.

These gloves are useless as gloves. They are capable, at most, of fulfilling the actual task of covering the hand only partially. Should we speak at best of a third category in light of such bold and in part virtuous structures, which have absolutely nothing in common with mittens or gloves? Of haute-couture gloves, as it were, produced for very special occasions, not for everyday use, which select, minimize, overdraw certain aspects, sometimes exaggerate trivialities, or are plain and radically simple?

Such gloves are unique pieces that question the common purpose and thereby shift other themes to the forefront: For example, the way that the materials are joined. Or they thematize the relationship of hand and glove, ask – architecturally – about the relationship of the cover to the enclosed space, about how a conglomerate of large and small units can be spatially encompassed and spanned.

Whereas the rationalists of the 1920s – to stay with the picture – sought the mitten, a form that allowed for a great deal, the functionalists aspired for the glove, the best possible use for the concrete case. In the words of Adolf Behne: "While the functionalist seeks the greatest adaptation to the most highly specialized function, the rationalist seeks the accommodation of many cases. They are those who want the most appropriate and unique for the particular case, and those who aspire to build what is fitting for general need, the norm" (*The Modern Functional Building*, 1926). The glove-objects arising from Professor Andrea Deplazes' chair withdraw, for the most part, from such attempts at categorization, but in a similar way, and meticulously, follow an architectonic-constructive idea.

The First Time

Christoph Elsener

It is not yet evening and you are asked to disassemble into pieces the work that you put together over the day. Before you go home, you carefully lay out the still wet clay parts to dry, not knowing that the next work day you will prepare them again, of another material, of cardboard. You have one day's time to reproduce them exactly and precisely, to then, on the following day, fill them – completed as small molds – with liquid plaster. To lay bare the dry plaster parts, you have to entirely destroy the cardboard pieces. You are then meant to compile the plaster pieces, according to a strategy of your own devices, to a new whole and fasten it with glue. Trial and error determine your decisions, making and thinking are the poles of your scope of action. The following day, you re-build your structure twice as large, load-bearing, out of wood beams. One day later again, you will supplement a part of your framework with cardboard slices and transparent paper, to define spaces and spatial transitions. A constant transformation runs like a red line through your works – in an alternation of destroying and re-making, changing and leaving, abandoning and gaining. A connection begins to emerge between decisions, rules, material, and space, between your will and its effects on your architectonic objects. You document your work with sketches and photographs.

A few weeks have passed since the very first day when you produced a glove or a chair out of two materials, and already you are busy planning a small building whose structure arises from a construction material of your choice. Your objects now gain a representative meaning, additional to the original; they become models, and at the same time, are without scale, one-to-one, but also signify something else, something greater.

With the intensified study of select built reference objects, you develop further possible relations of material, structure, and space. Your presentations are continually discussed and evaluated. In the end, over the course of several weeks you create a constructive project for a user of your own imagination at a site of your choice. You set the rules, all that is assigned to you is the building material. The lecture, the lecture notes, and a series of seminars support you in formulating a substantial and harmonious concept. During the seminar week, working in a small group you choose from the alternatives to plan and carry out a structure of wood, cardboard, or metal.

This is your first year in "1:1-Architecture". You turn the partially poetic, partially odd or strictly architectural results of all your working steps into little spatial manifestos. And leave behind for us, the legacy of inspiration.

Urs Jeltsch Composition 1998–1999

Urszula Skoczylas Glove 2001–2002

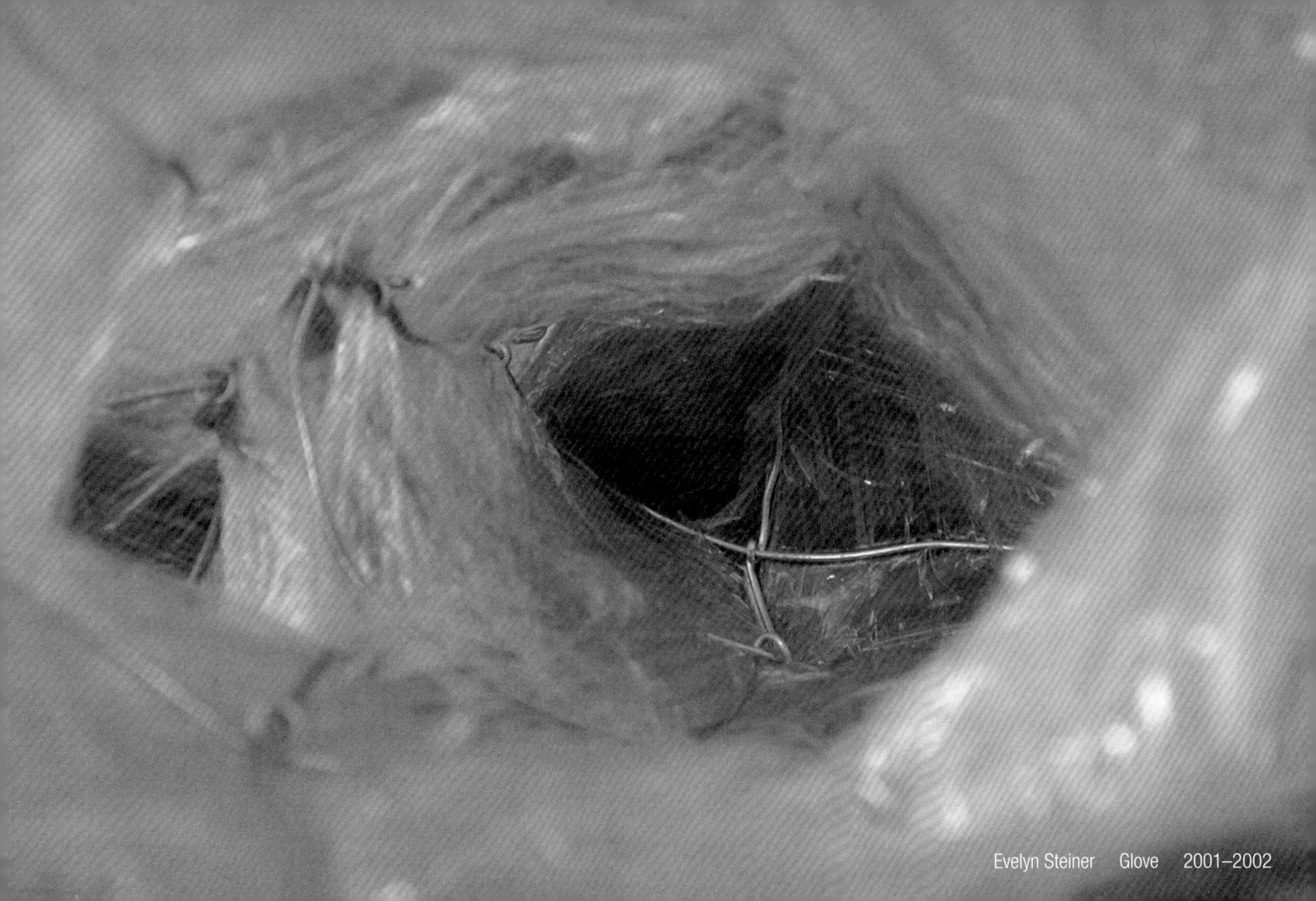

Evelyn Steiner Glove 2001–2002

Kaj Blattner Glove 2001–2002

Helen Wyss Glove 2001–2002

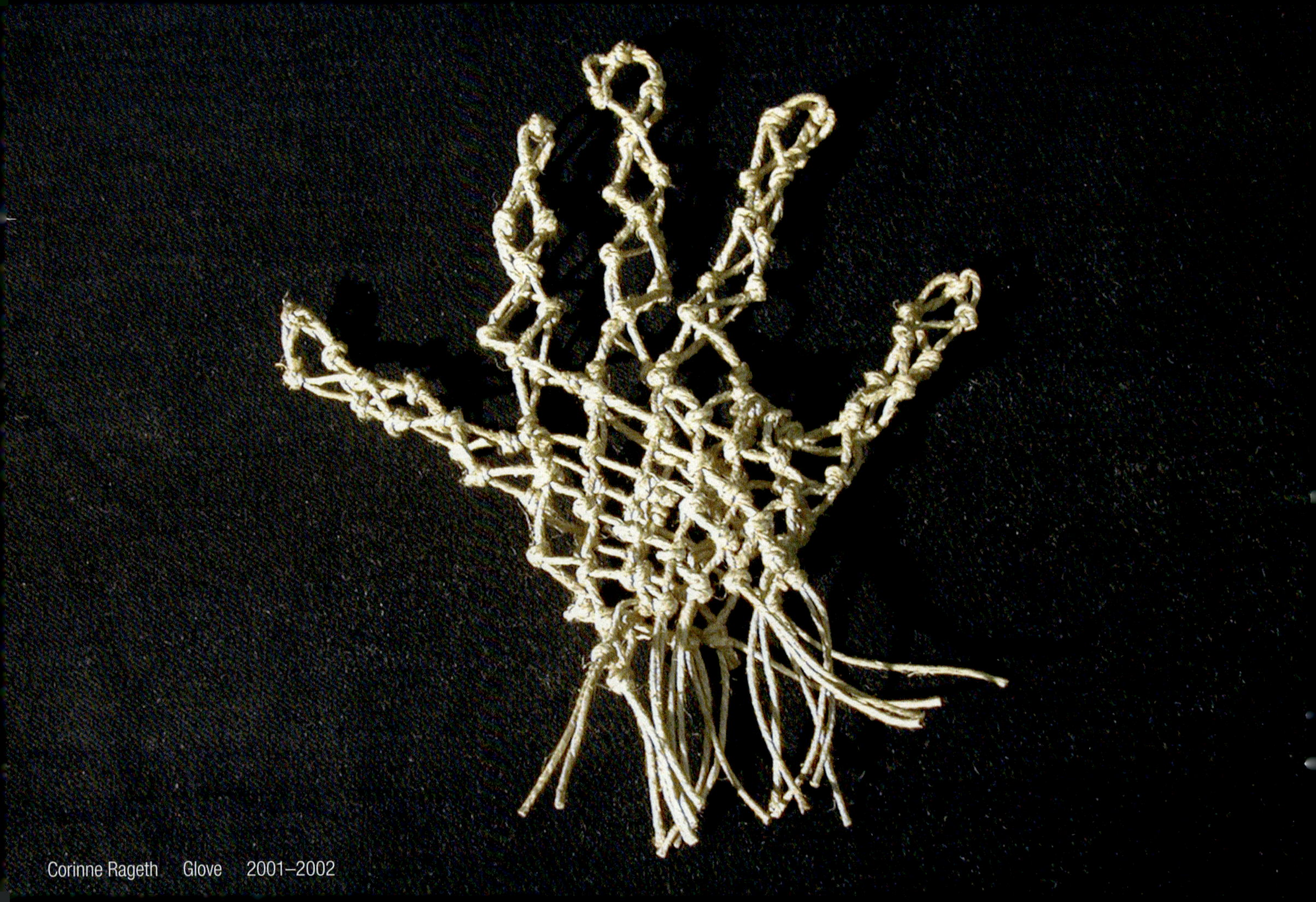

Corinne Rageth Glove 2001–2002

Unknown author Glove 2001–2002

Unknown author Tomography 1999–2000

Sandra Caminada Glove 2001–2002

Taichi Naito Glove 2003–2004

Christian Looser, Corinne Rageth Räumling 2001–2002

Alexander Menke, Dominique Wehrli   Composition   2000–2001

Unknown author   Transformation   2001–2002

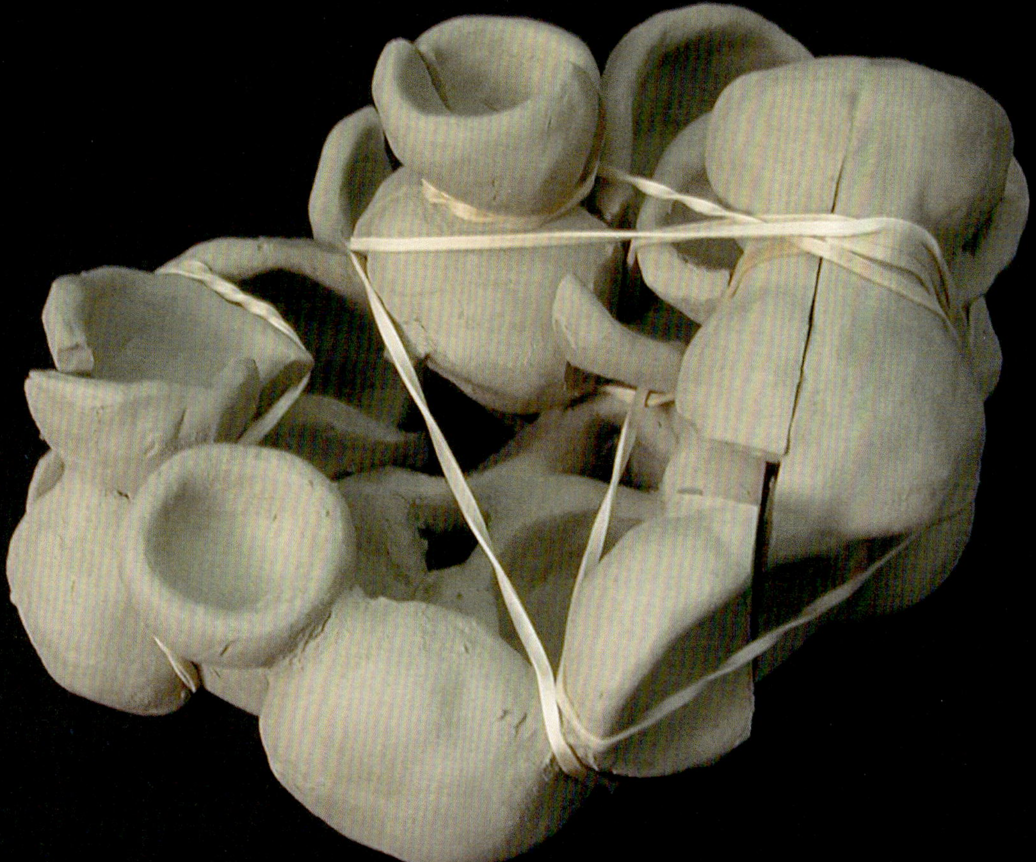

Unknown author Räumling 2001–2002

Adrian Fergg, Simon Fischer   Composition   2001–2002

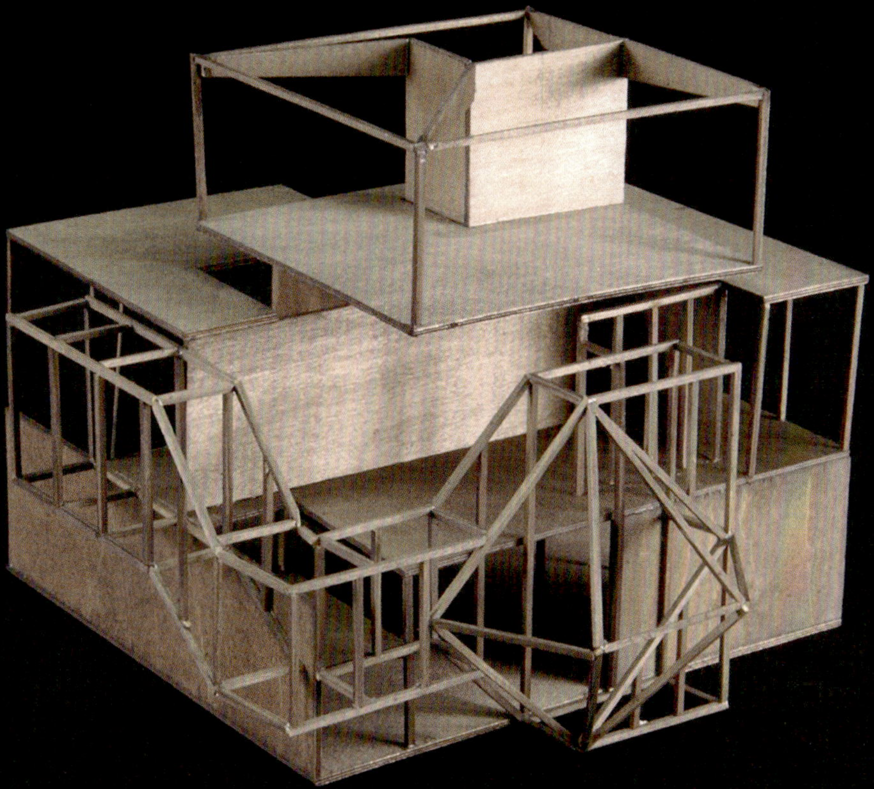

Adrian Fergg, Simon Fischer Tectonics 2001–2002

Martina Bisaz, Oliver Hongler   Structure   2001–2002

Martina Bisaz, Oliver Hongler Composition 2001–2002

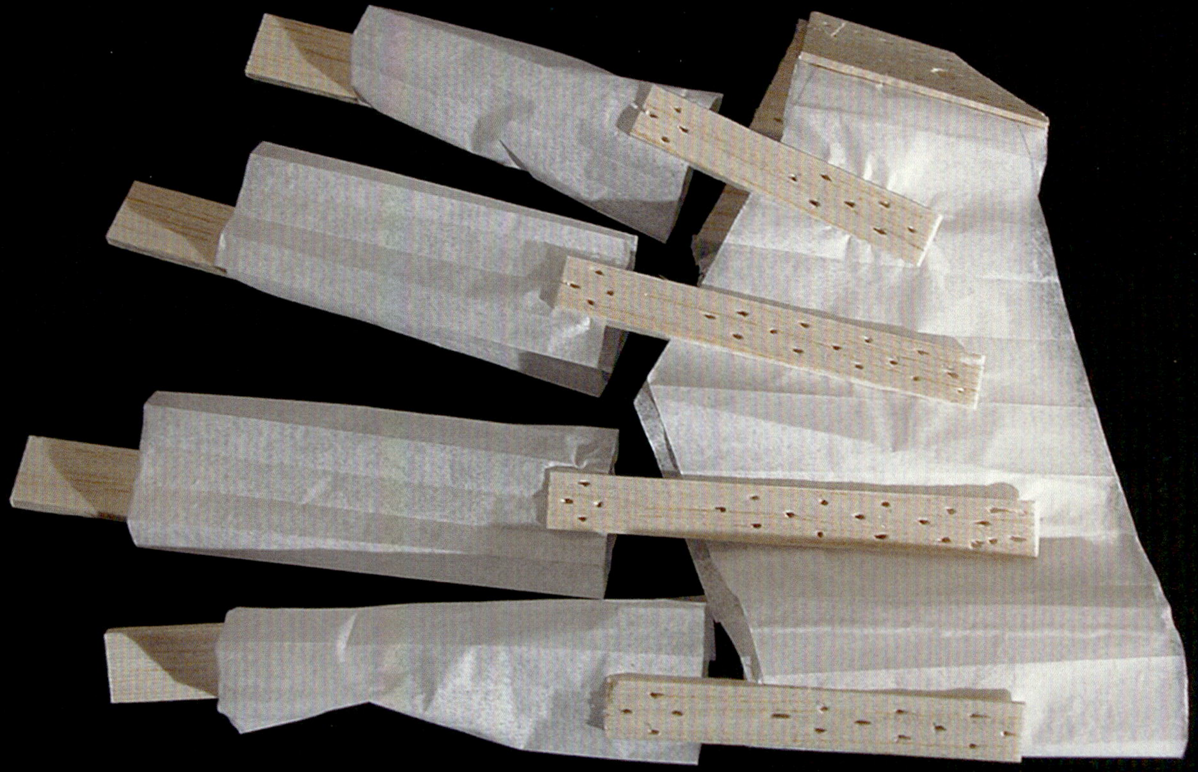

Darius Karácsony Glove 2003–2004

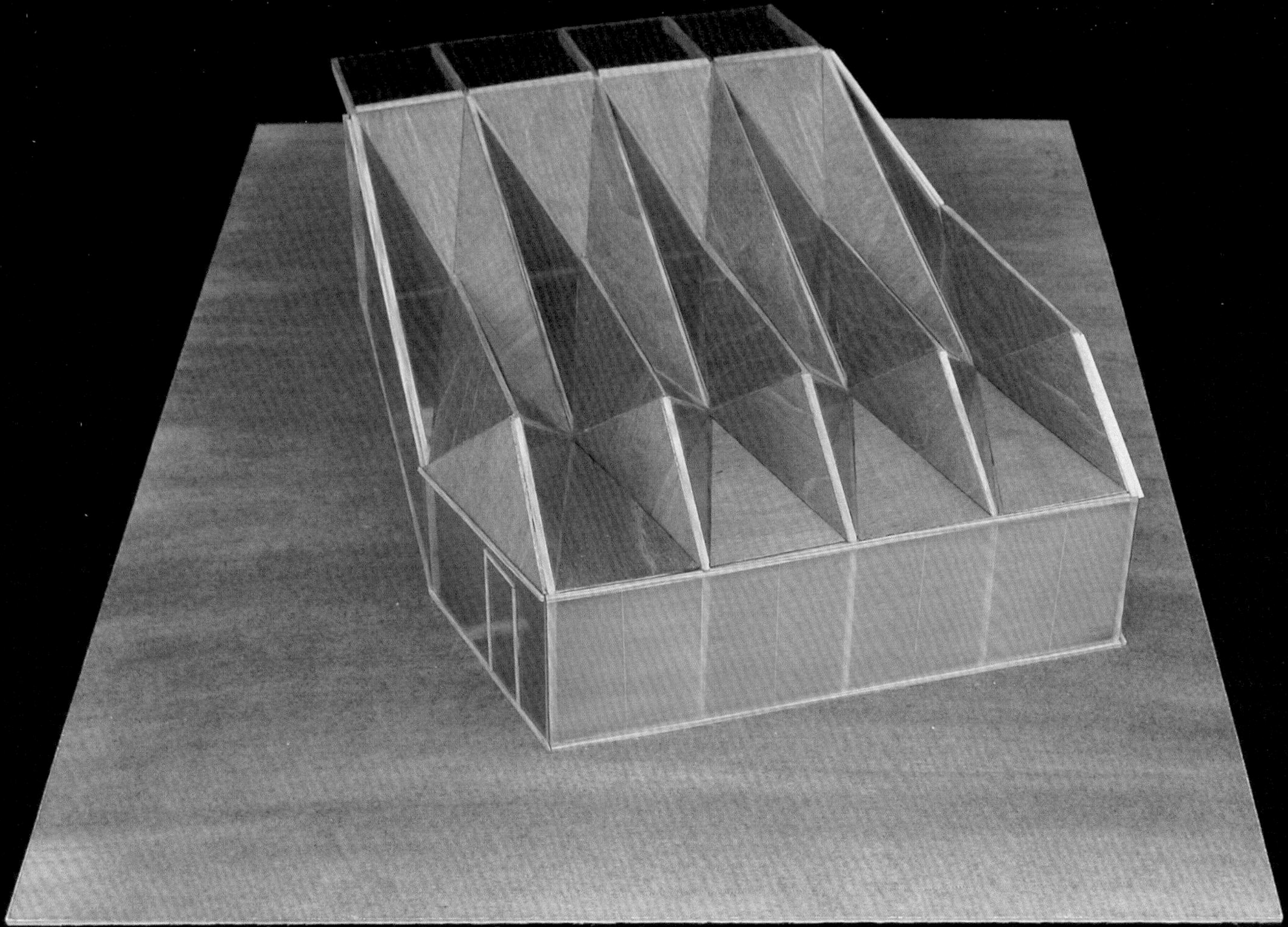

Stephan Bischof, Mauro Caviezel   Constructive project   2002–2003

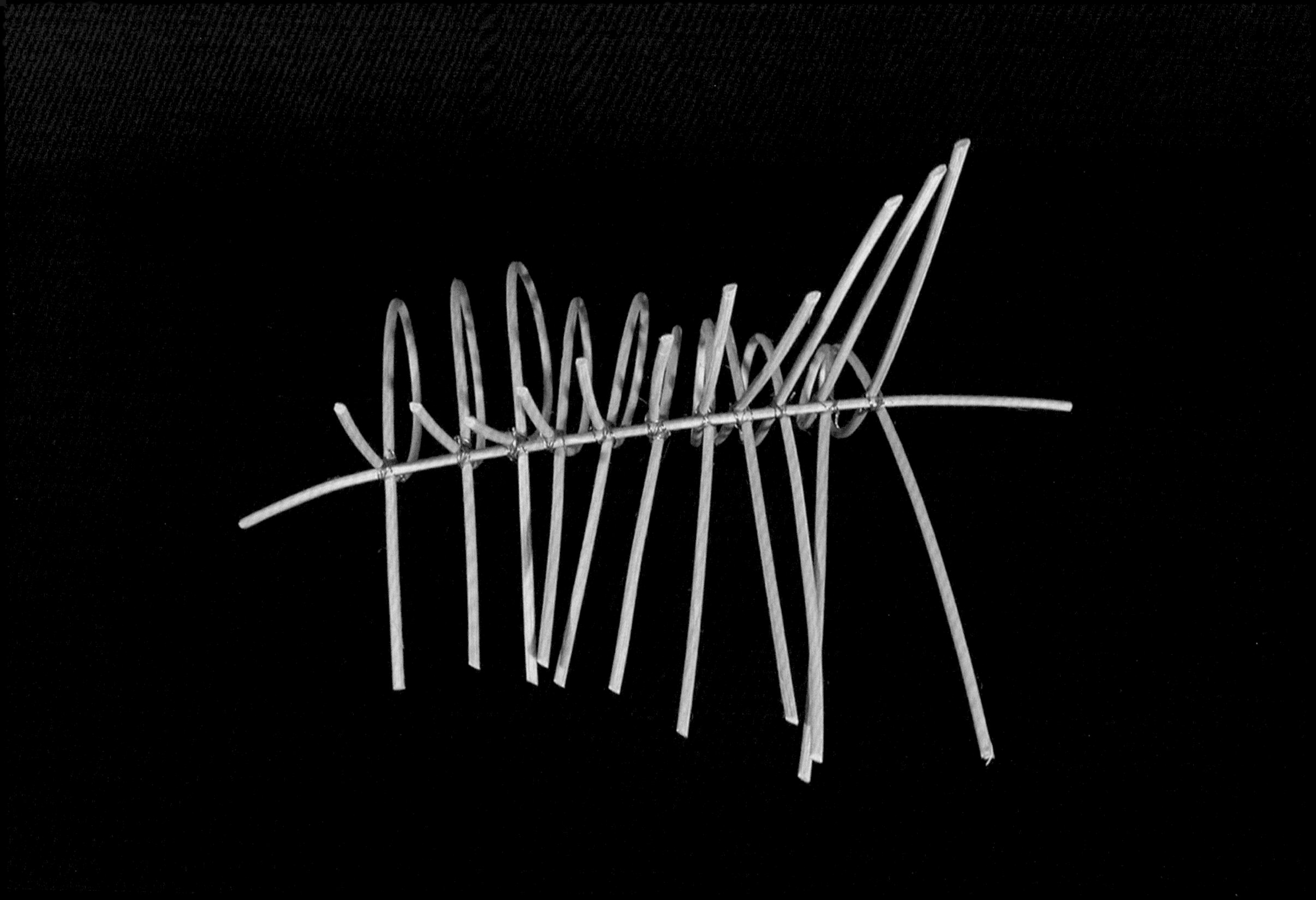

Lilian Schmid Glove 2003–2004

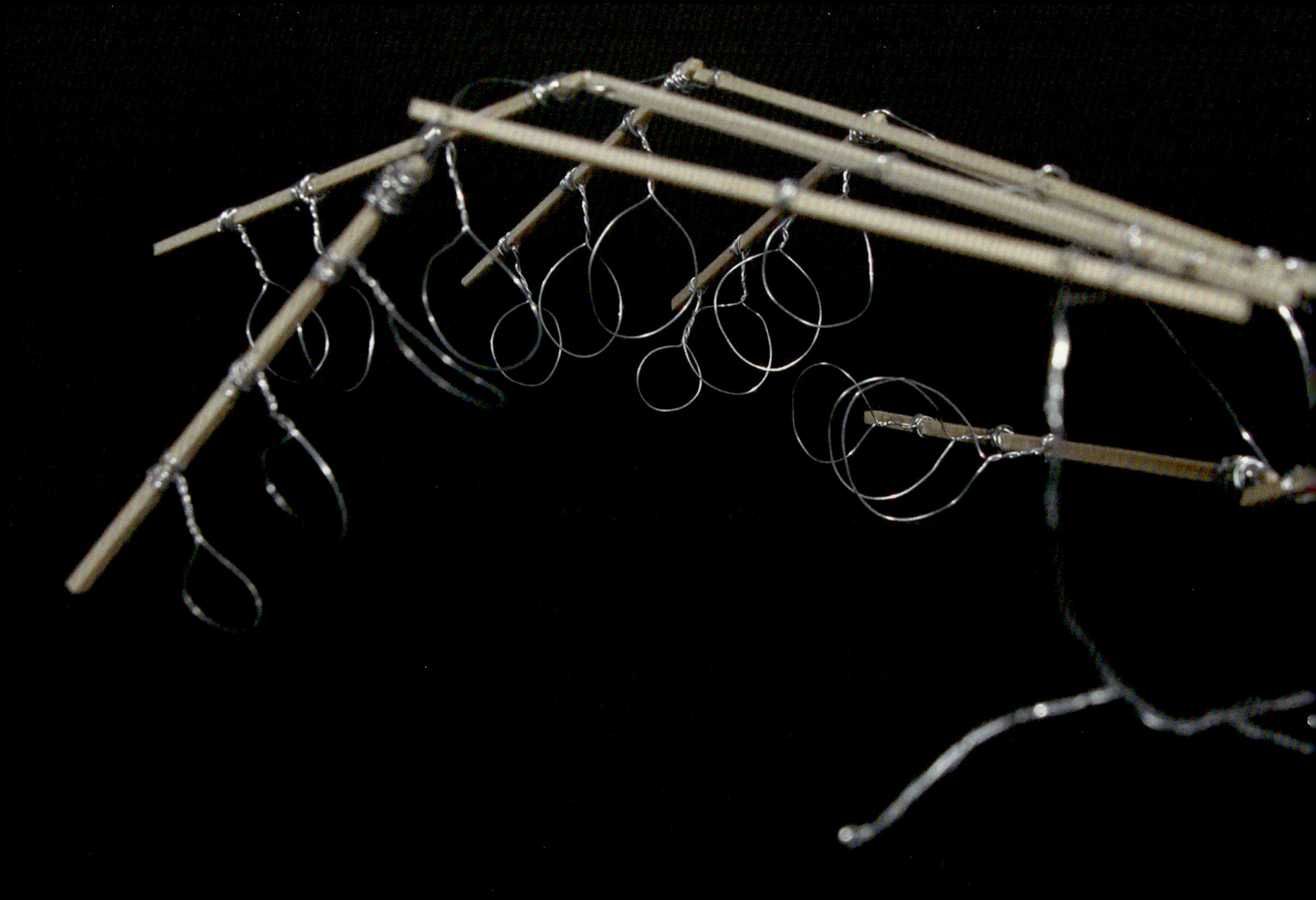

Flavia Sutter Glove 2003–2004

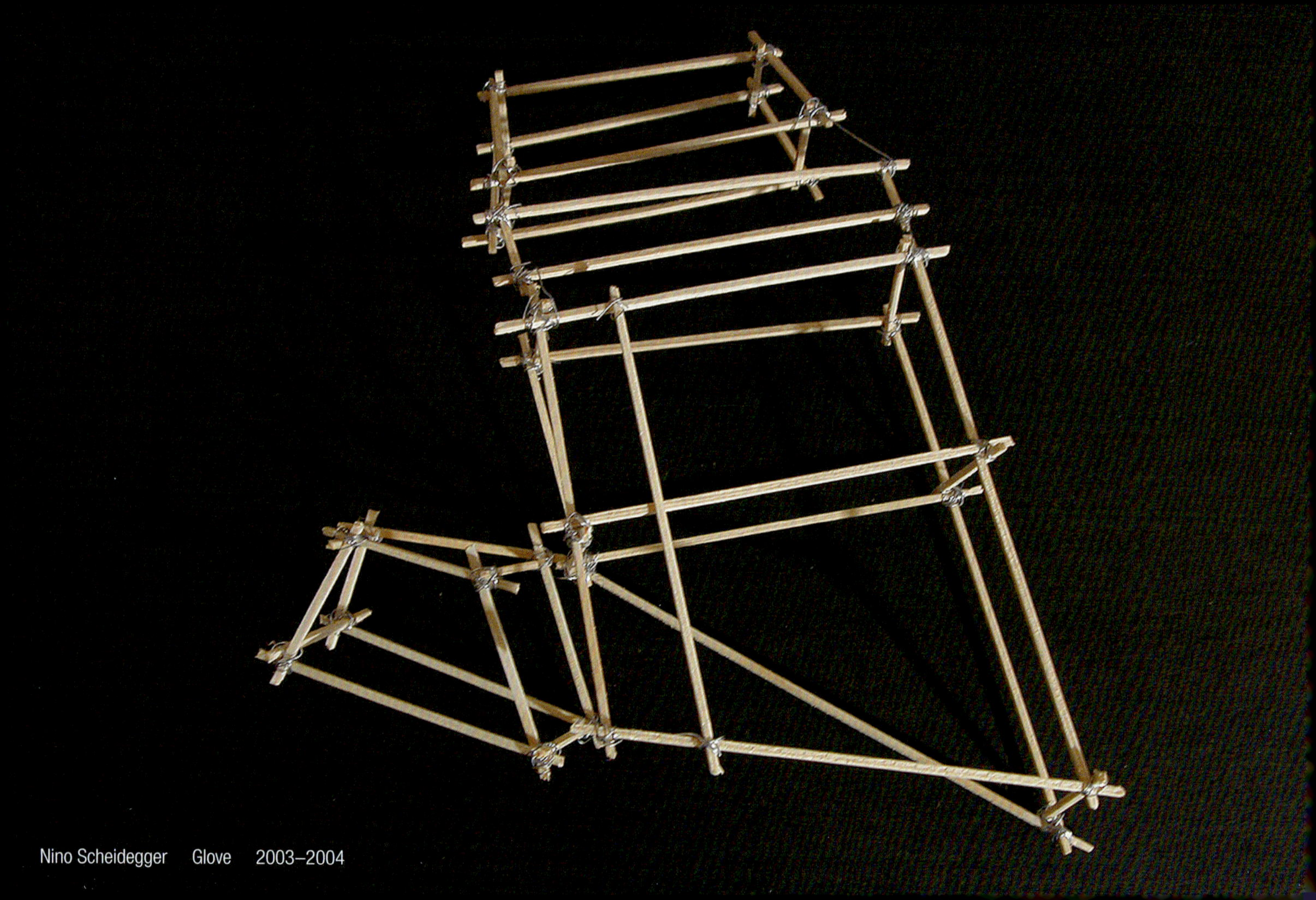

Nino Scheidegger Glove 2003–2004

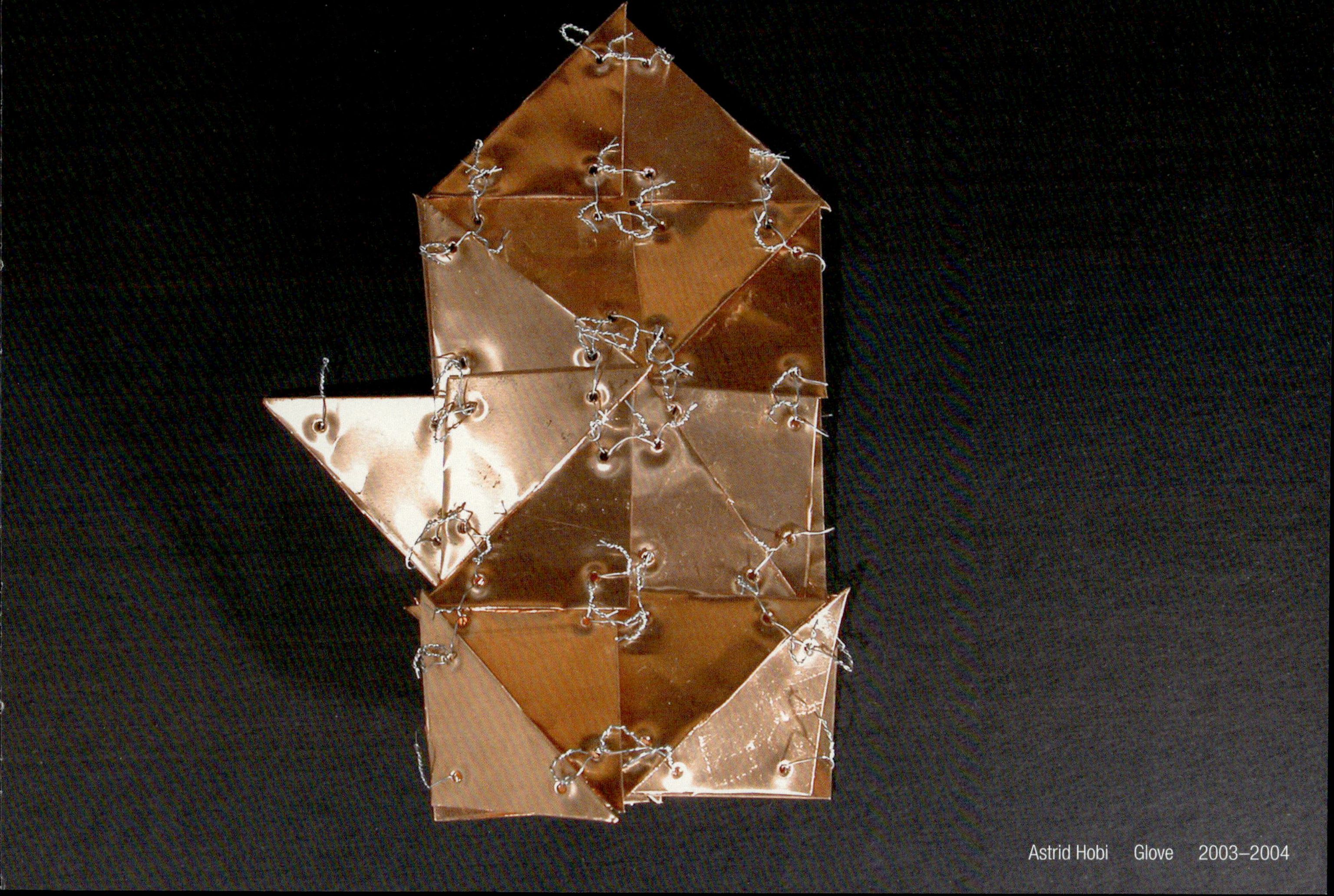

Astrid Hobi Glove 2003–2004

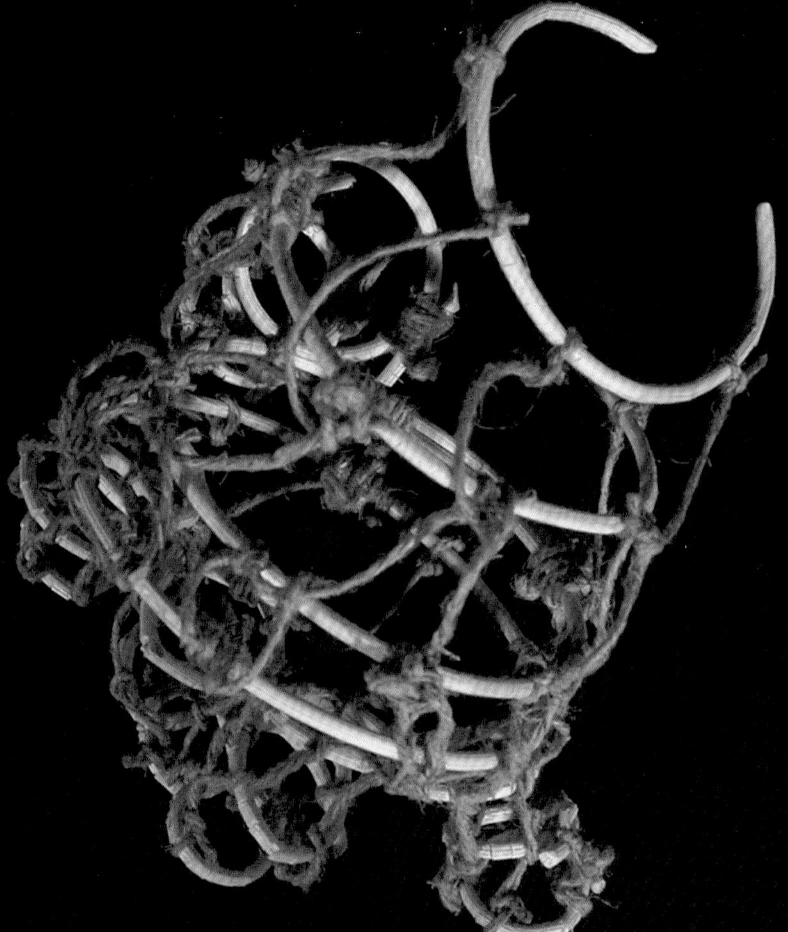

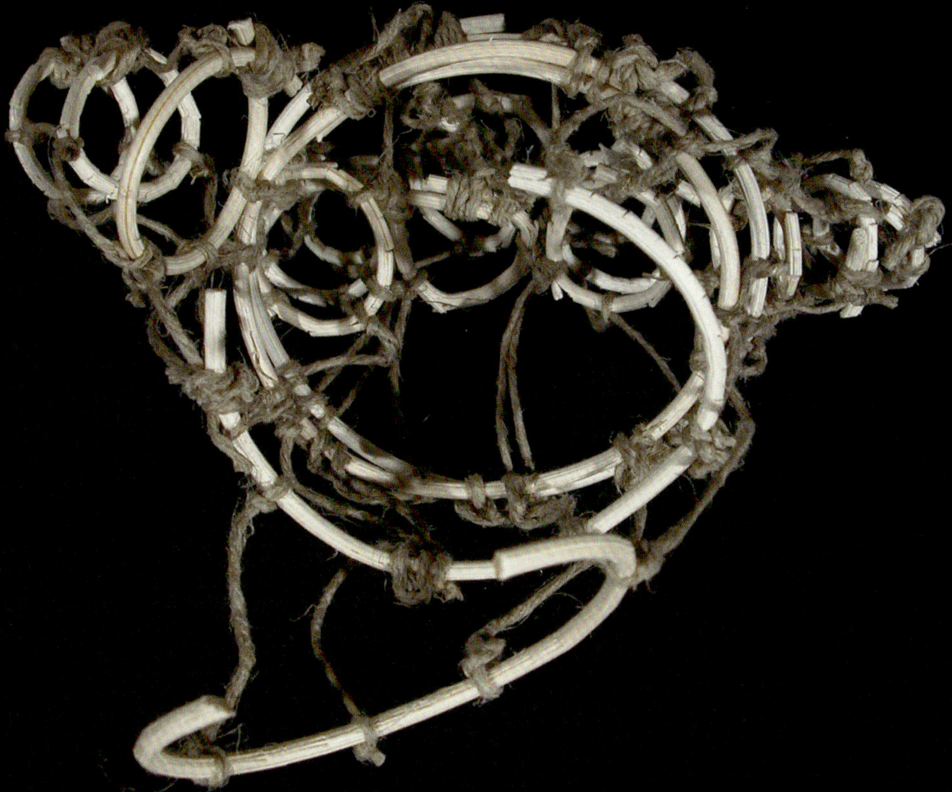

Melanie Stulz   Glove   2003–2004

Gregor Iten Glove 2003–2004

Martina Sutter Glove 2003–2004

Rebecca Inauen Glove 2003–2004

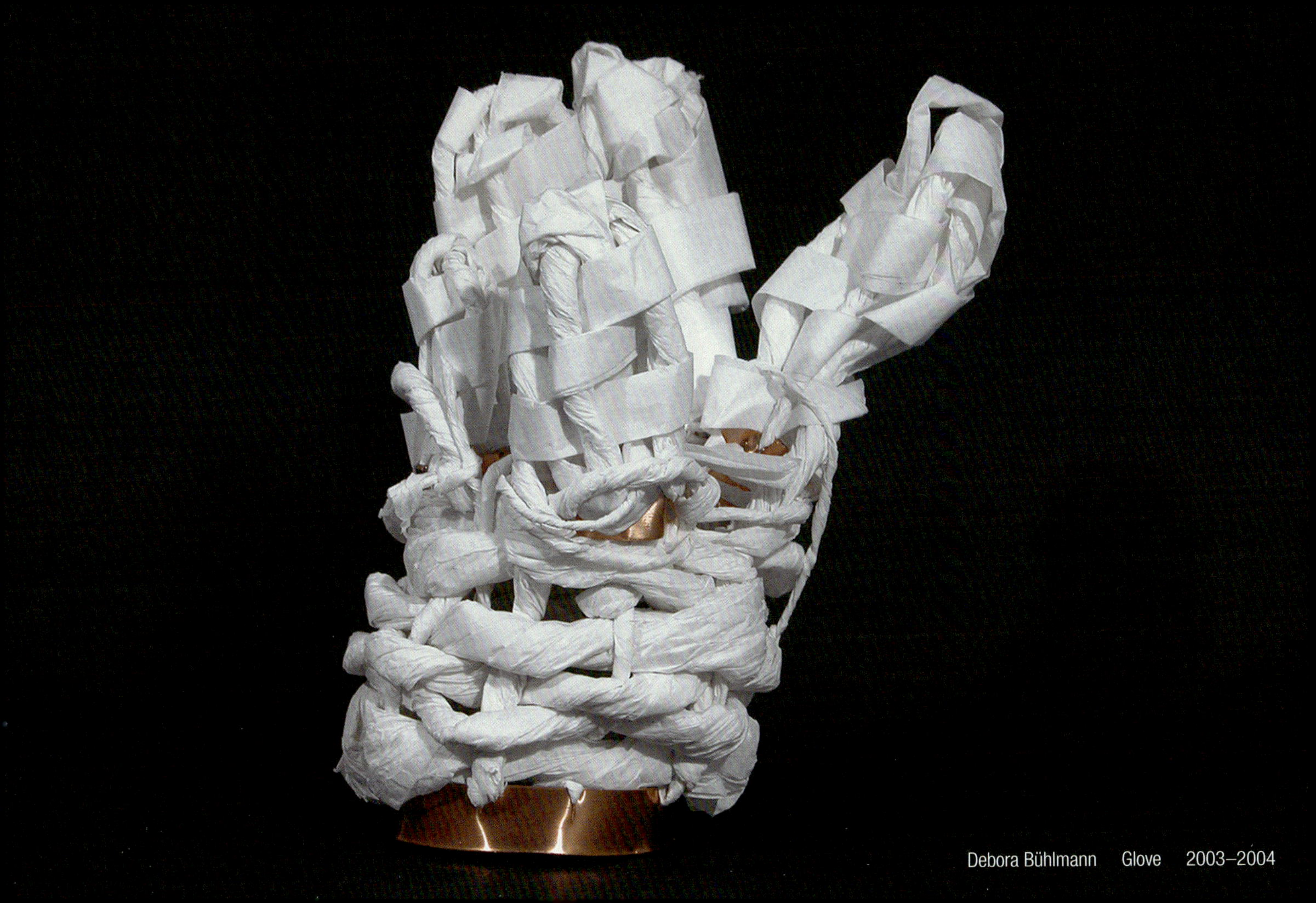

Debora Bühlmann Glove 2003–2004

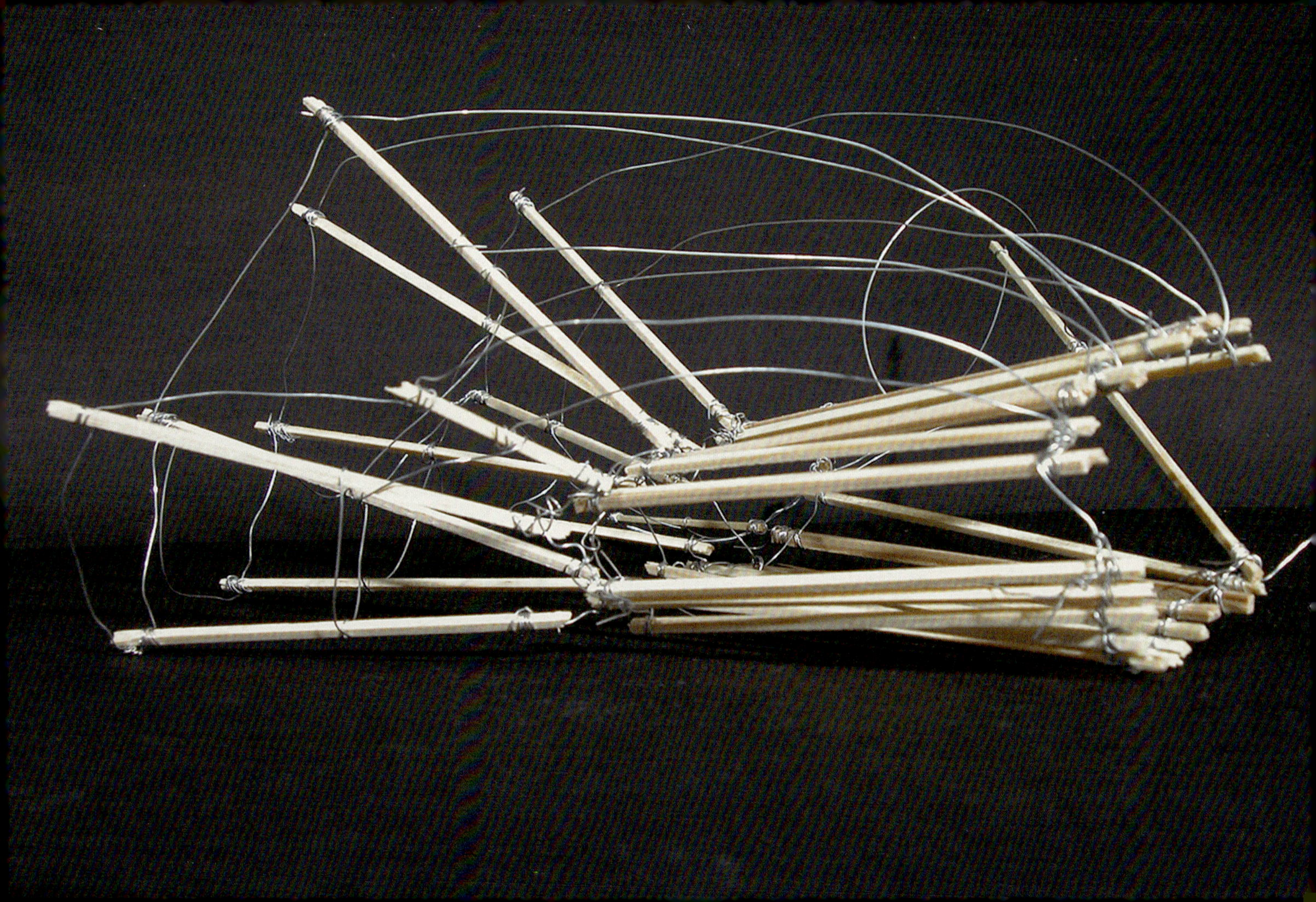

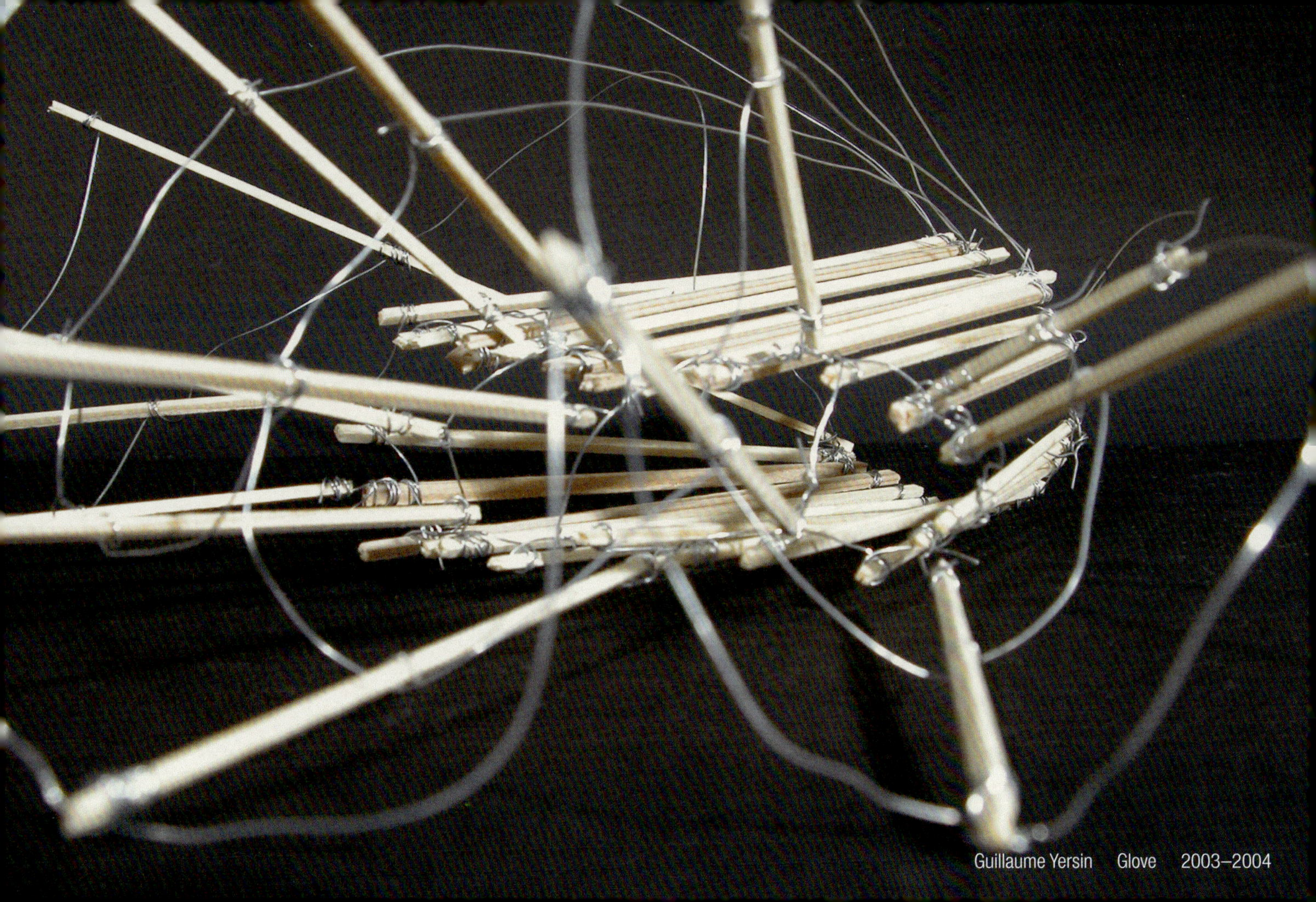

Guillaume Yersin Glove 2003–2004

Florian Grunder   Transformation   2003–2004

Florian Grunder Mold.Pouring 2003–2004

Regula Bischoff Mold.Pouring 2003–2004

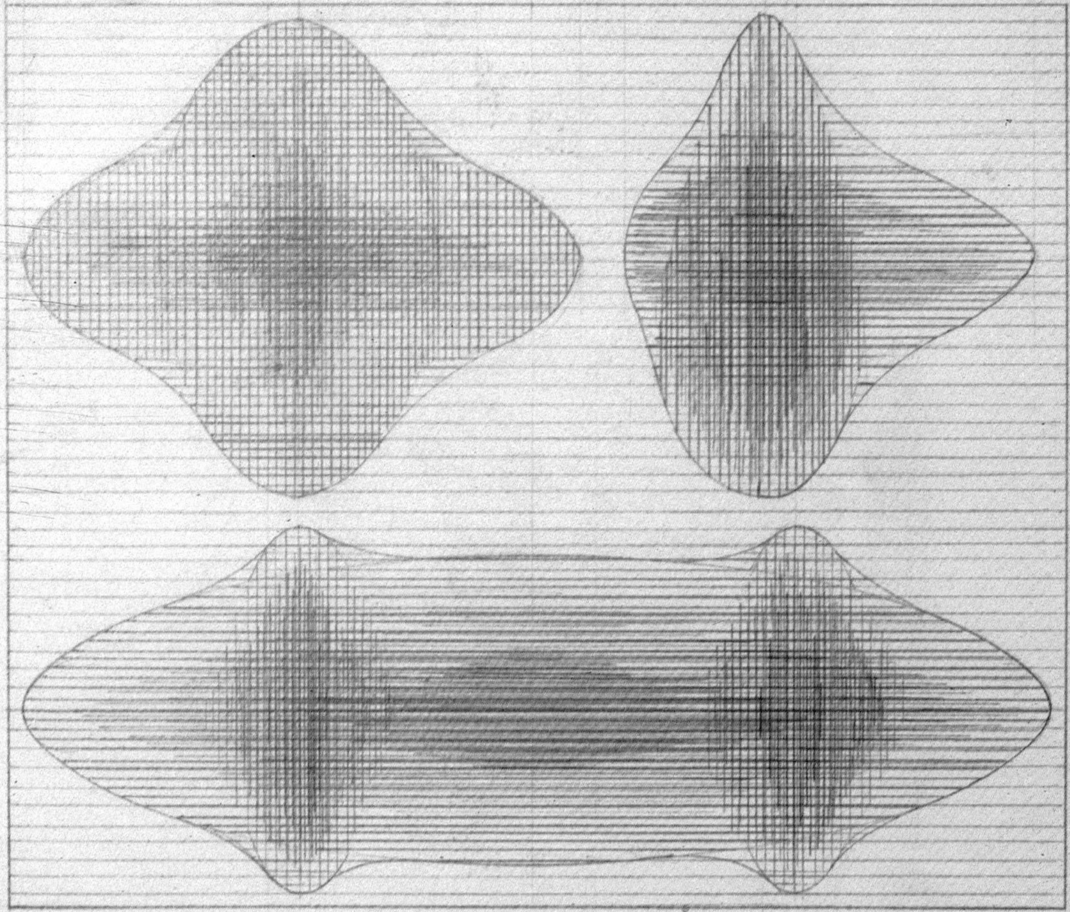

Gabriel Studerus Tomography 1998–1999

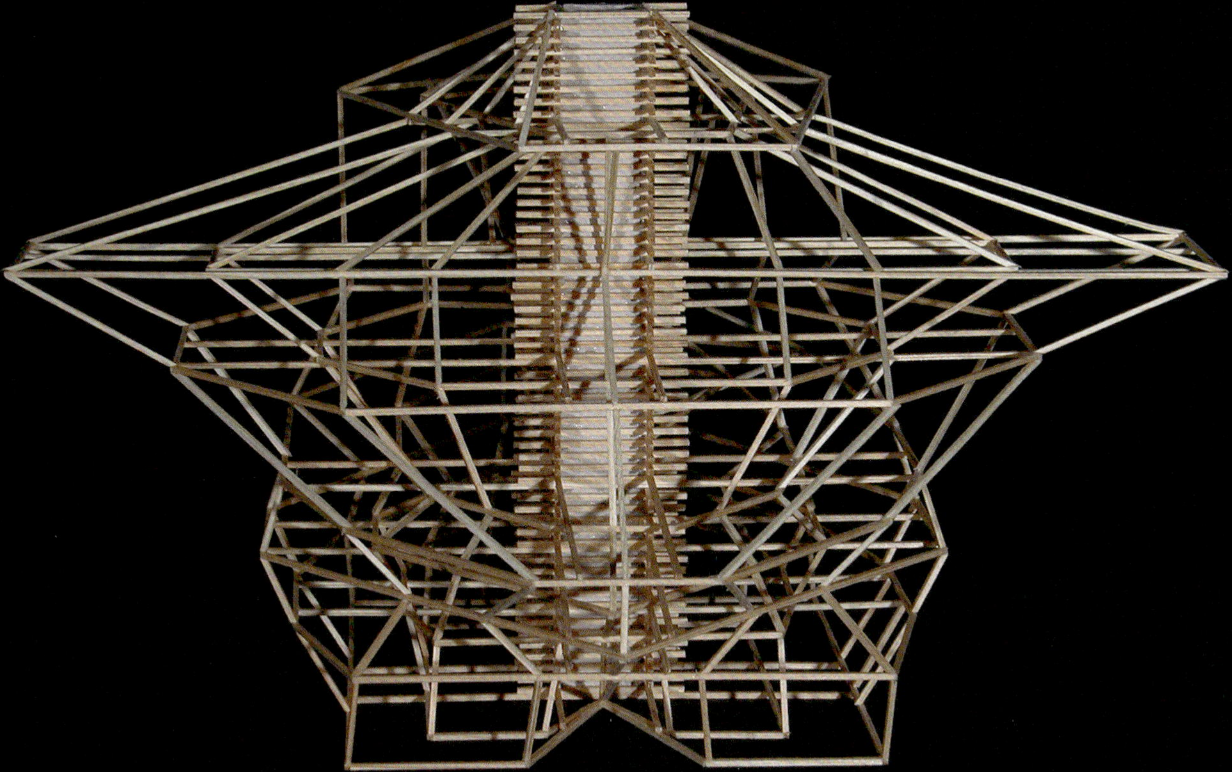

Jin-Woo Lee, Tamara Prader Structure 2003–2004

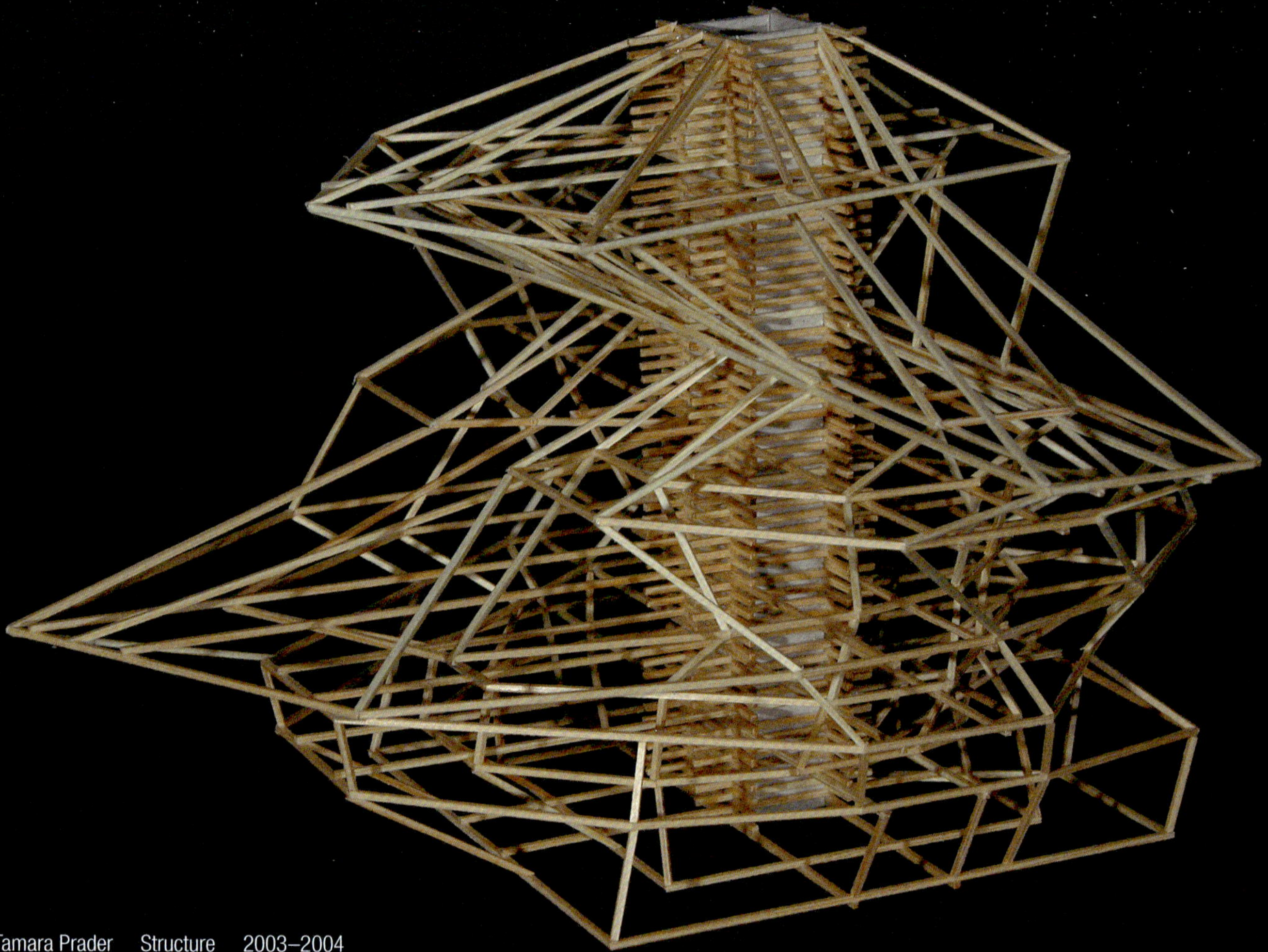

Jin-Woo Lee, Tamara Prader   Structure   2003–2004

Philip Bräm, Stefan Moser   Constructive project   2000–2001

Jens Gerber, Nicolas Guex Constructive project 2003–2004

Adrian Meier, Lukas Vogt Constructive project 2003–2004

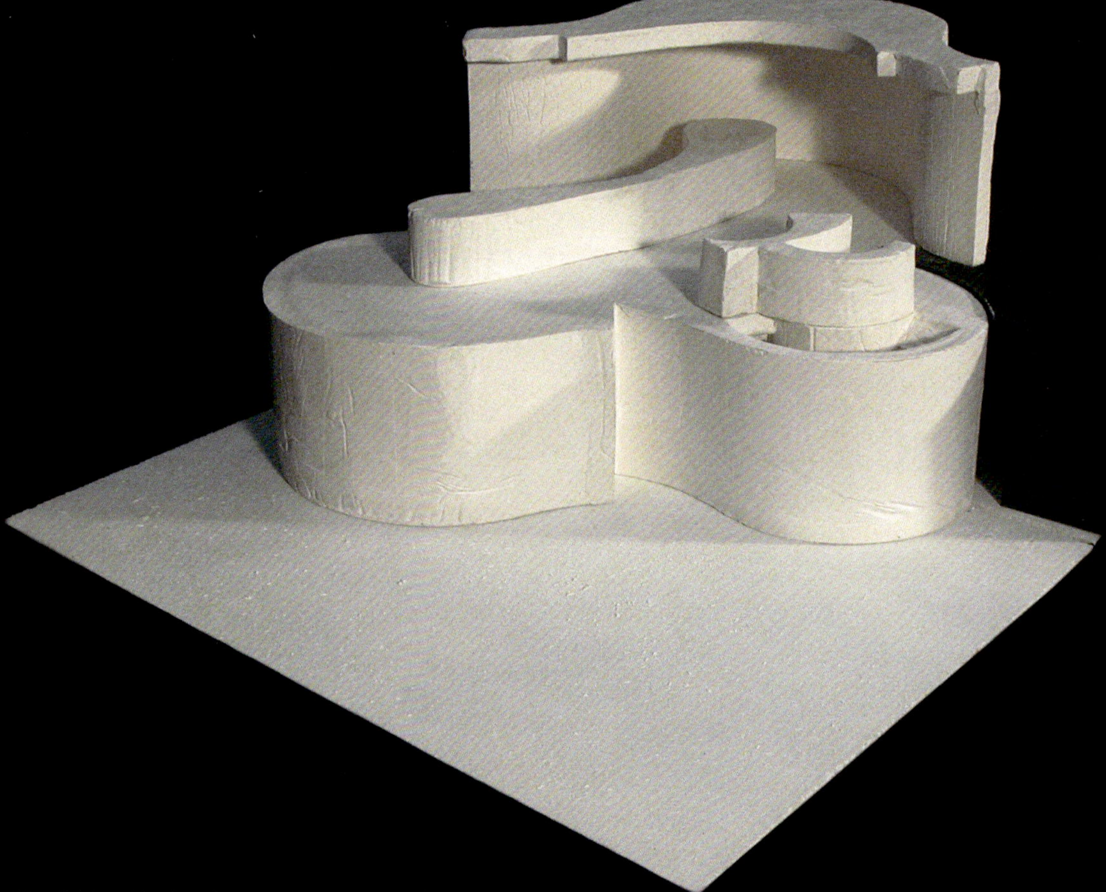

Nicolas Burckhardt, Harry Heyck Constructive project 2004–2005

Esther Steube, Daniela Weber Constructive project 2004–2005

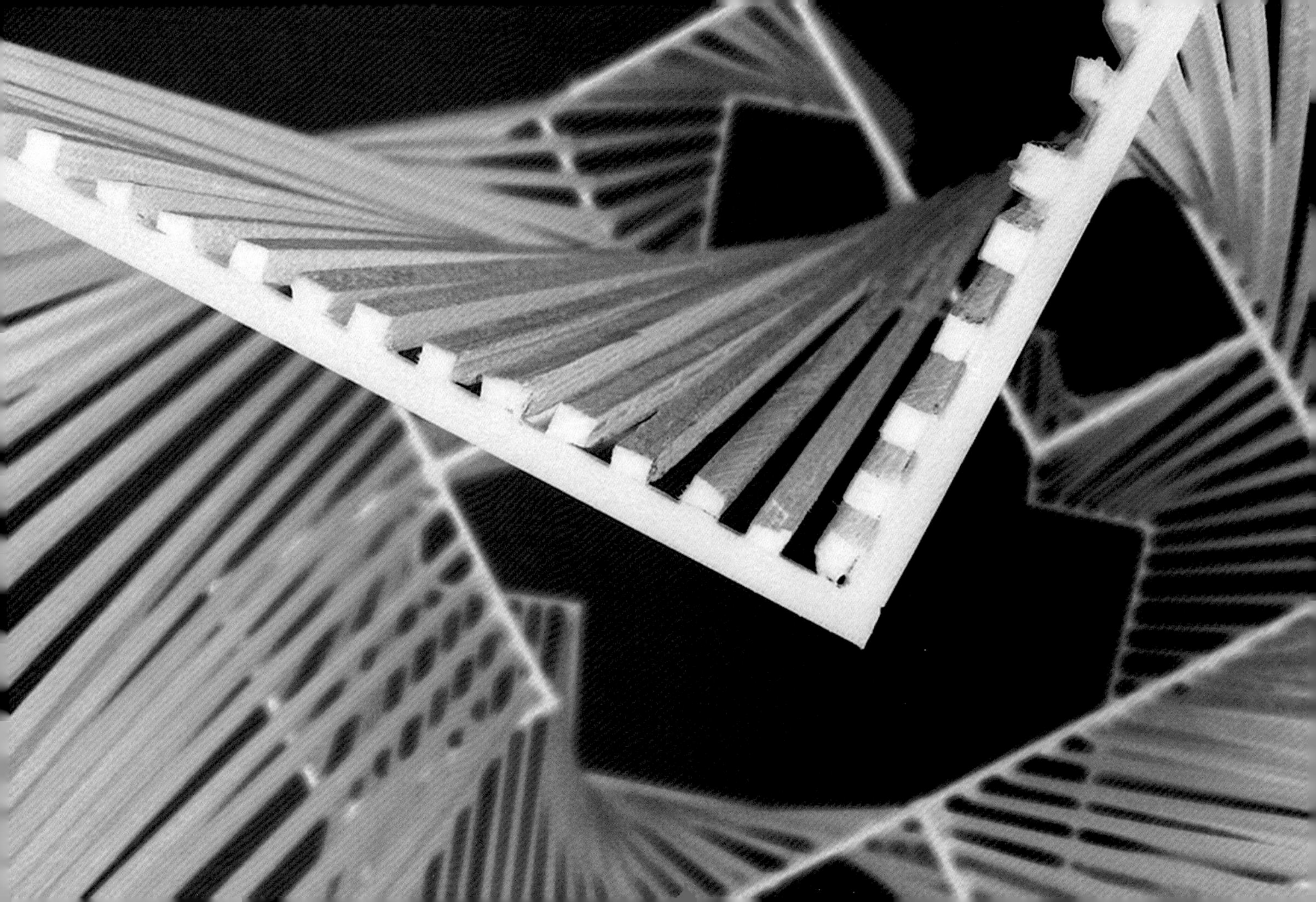

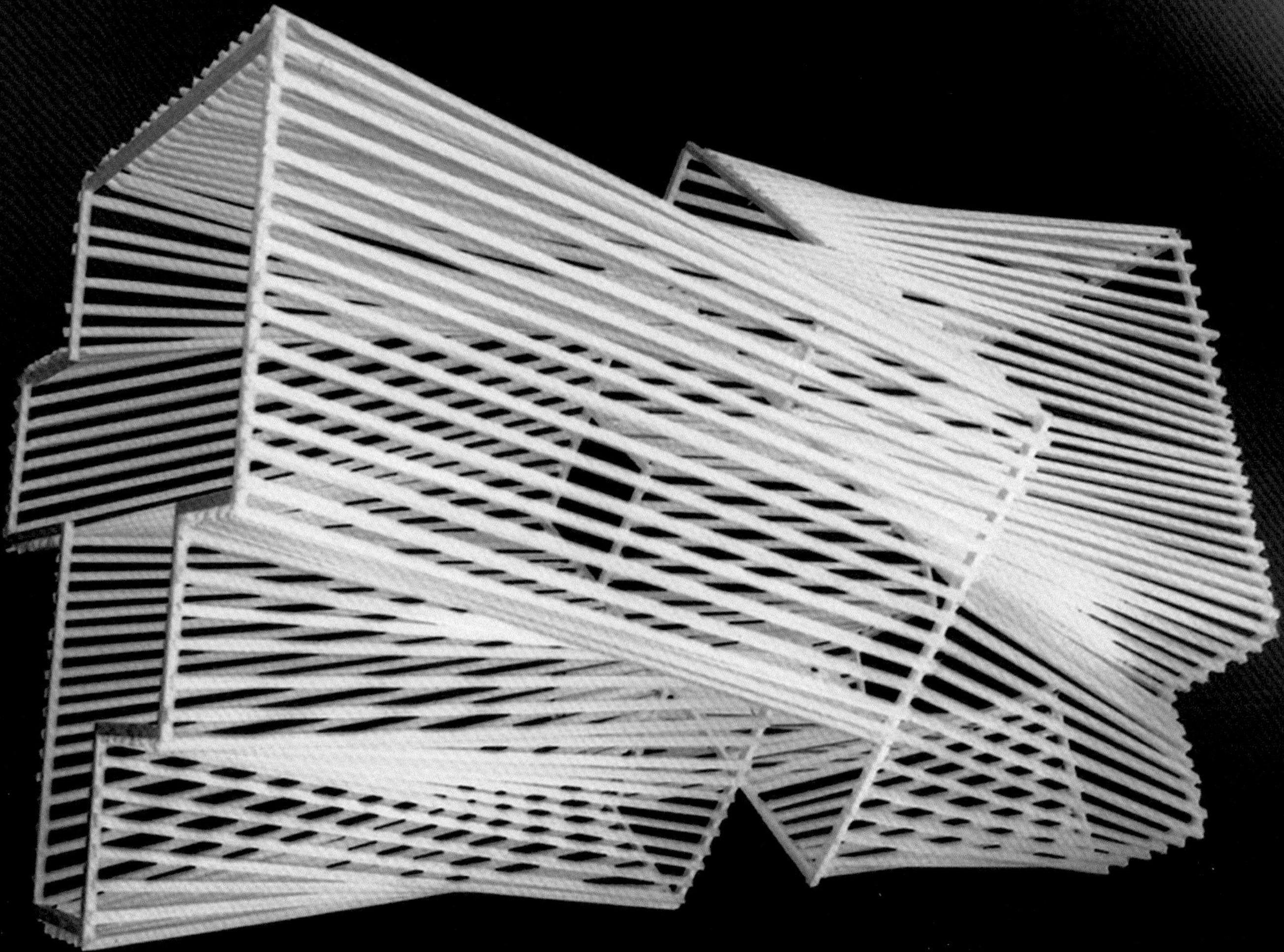

Stefan Diethelm, Fabian Landolt Structure 2004–2005

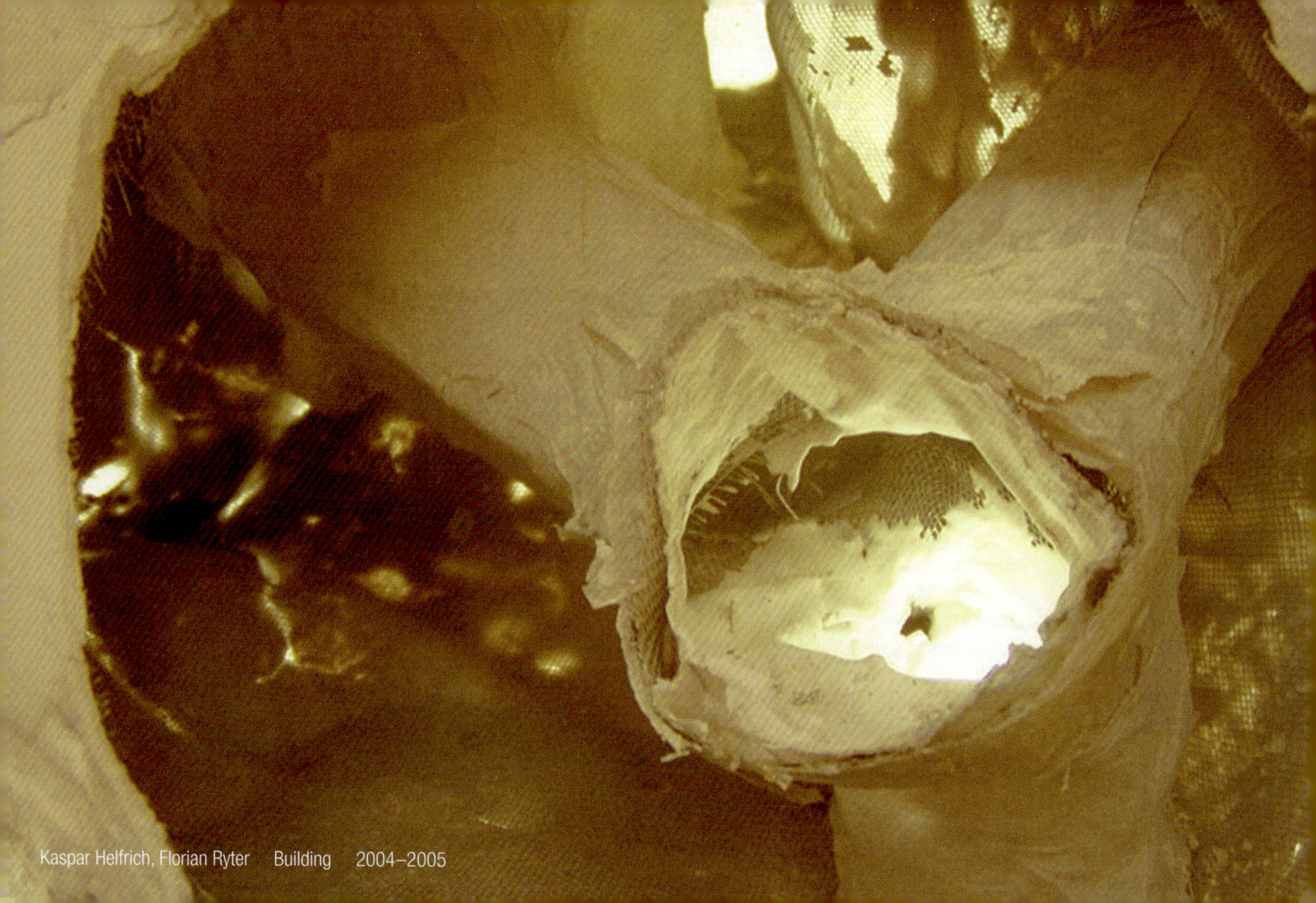
Kaspar Helfrich, Florian Ryter   Building   2004–2005

Jens Jaschek, Lea Walzer   Building   2004–2005

Silvio Bühlmann, Stephan Sturzenegger Space 2004–2005

Silvio Bühlmann, Stephan Sturzenegger Building 2004–2005

Frederic Schwarz, Robert Wäschenfelder Structure 2004–2005

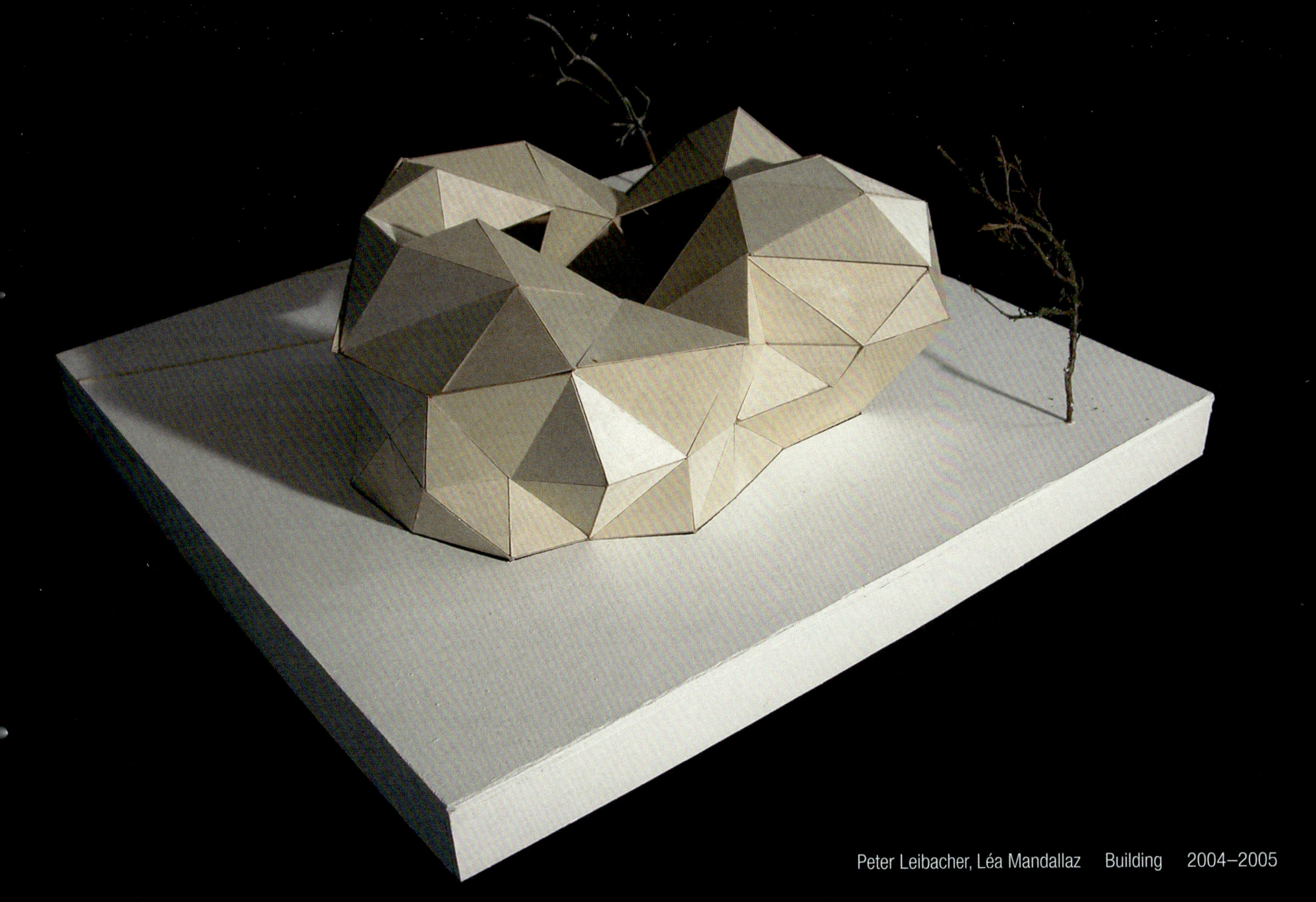

Peter Leibacher, Léa Mandallaz Building 2004–2005

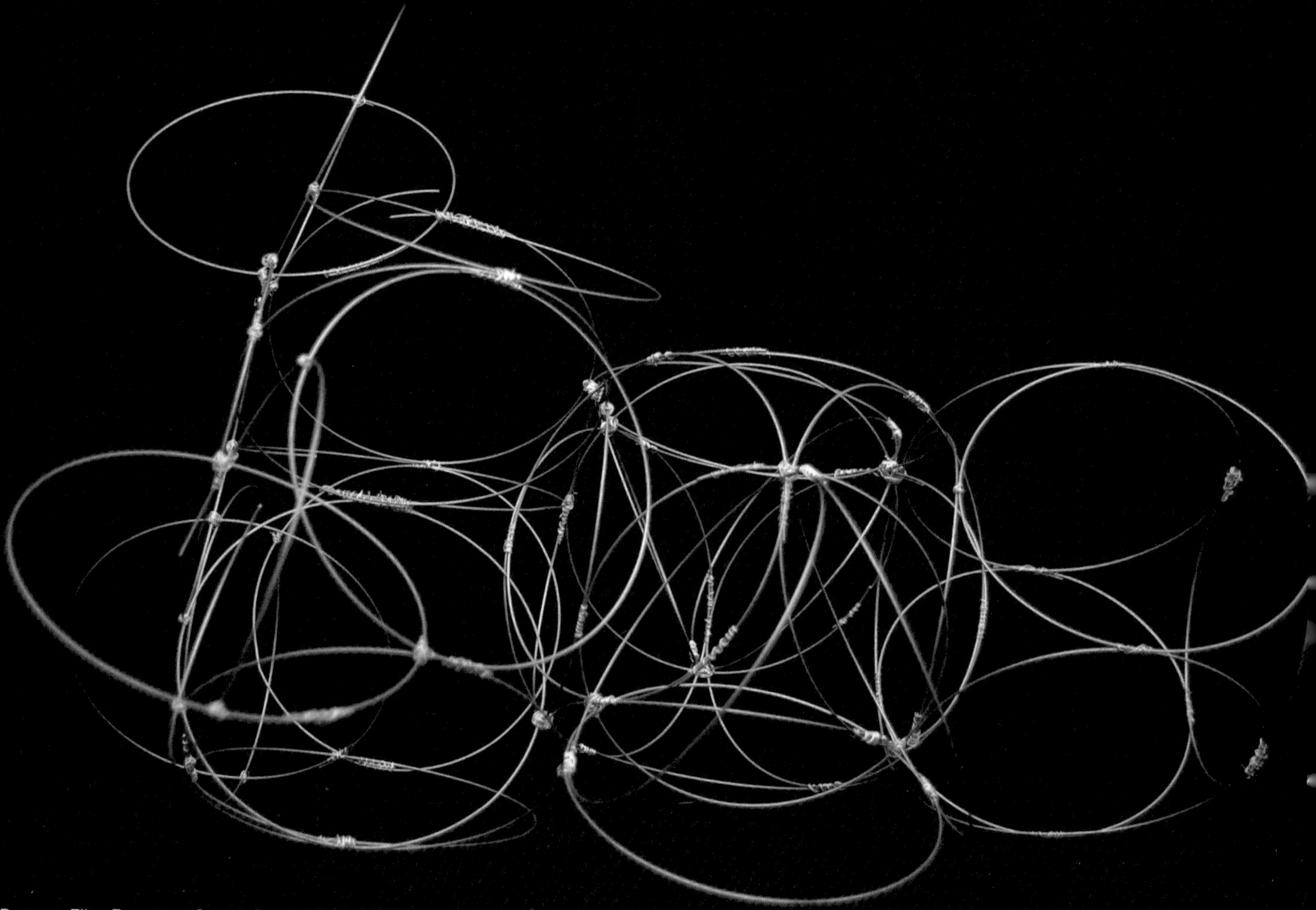

Silvana Brunner, Elisa Ferraro   Connection   2005–2006

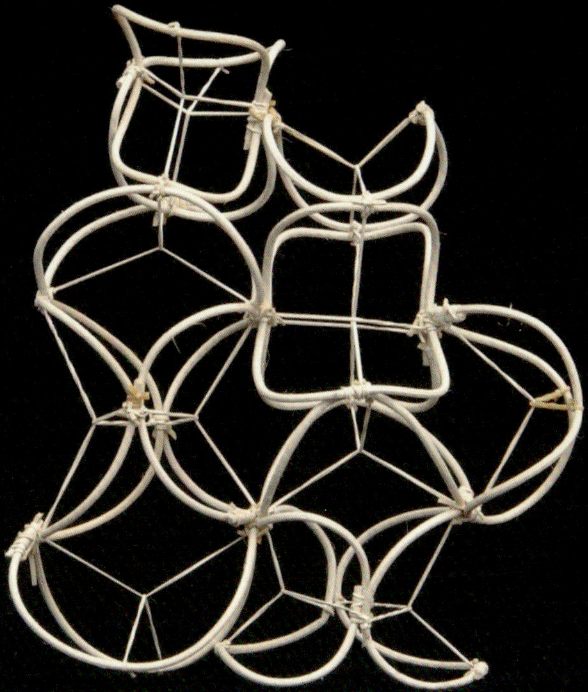

Unknown author Connection 2005–2006

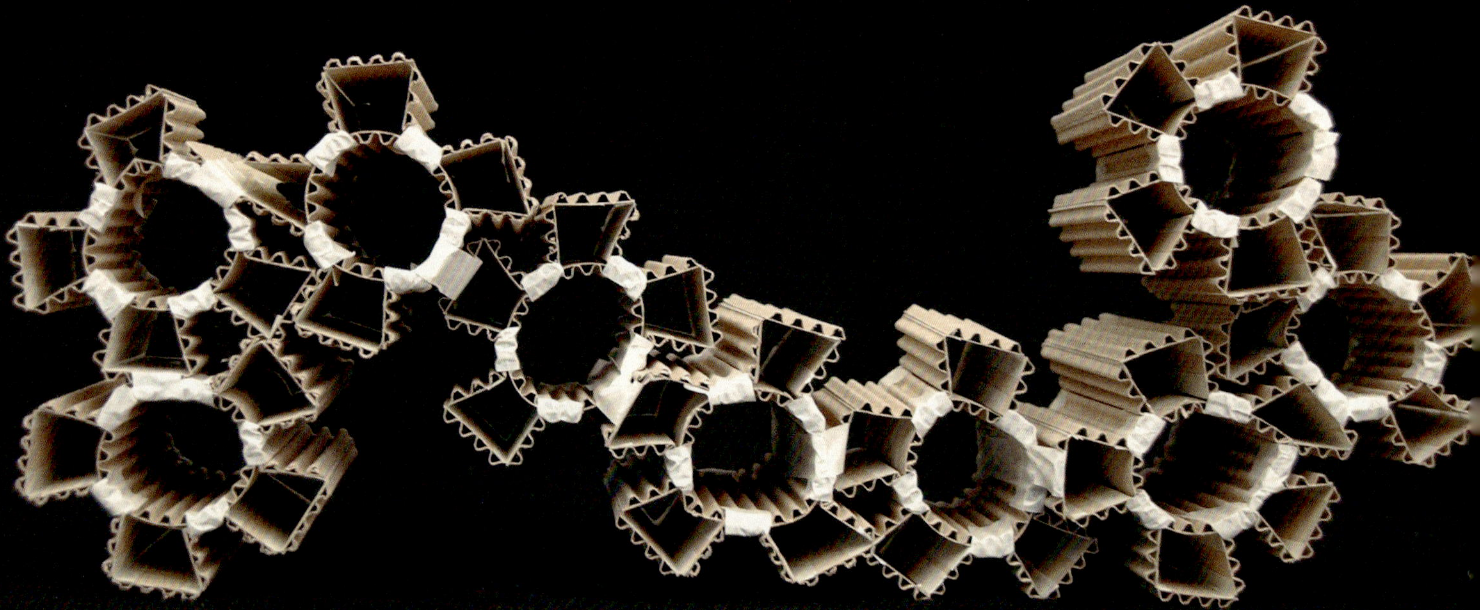

Unknown author Connection 2005–2006

Isabelle Meister, Milena Vuletic   Connection   2005–2006

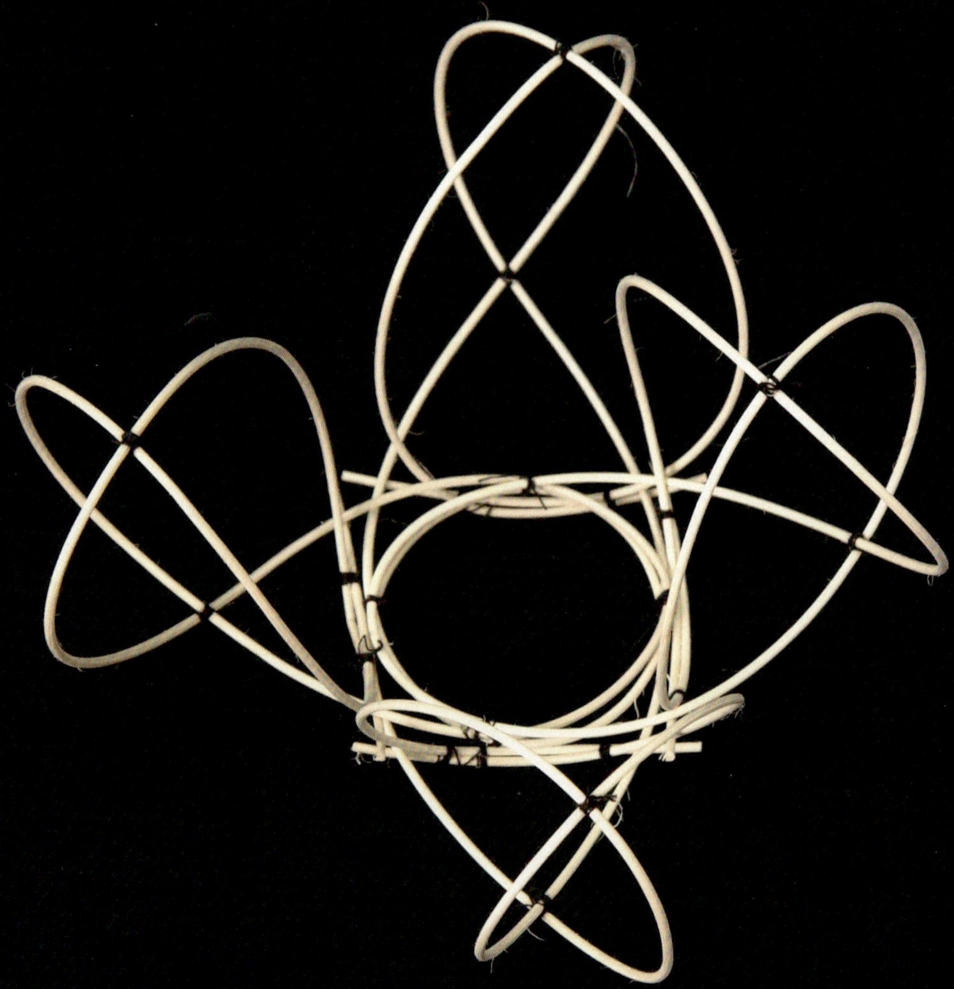

Unknown author Connection 2005–2006

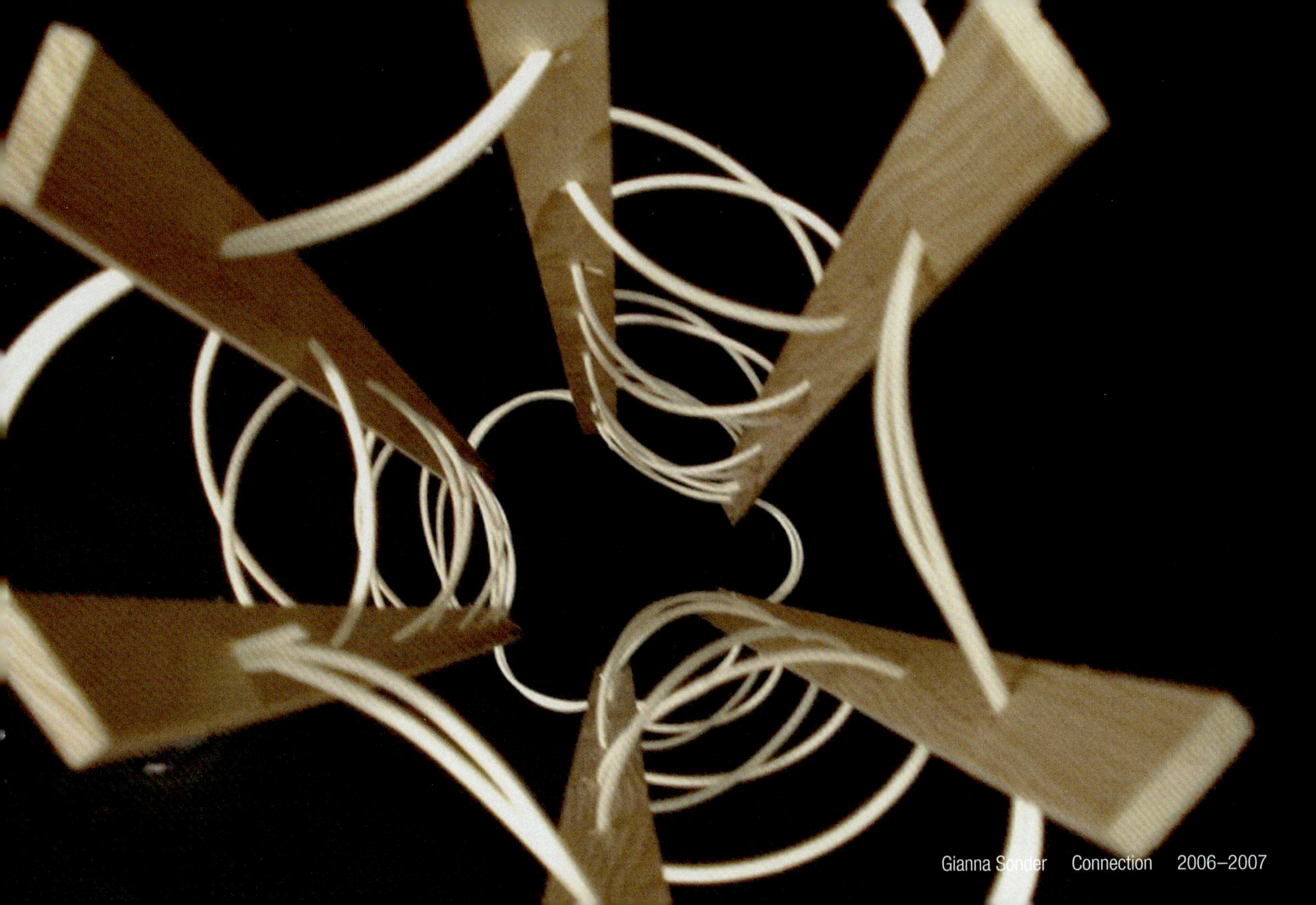

Gianna Sonder Connection 2006–2007

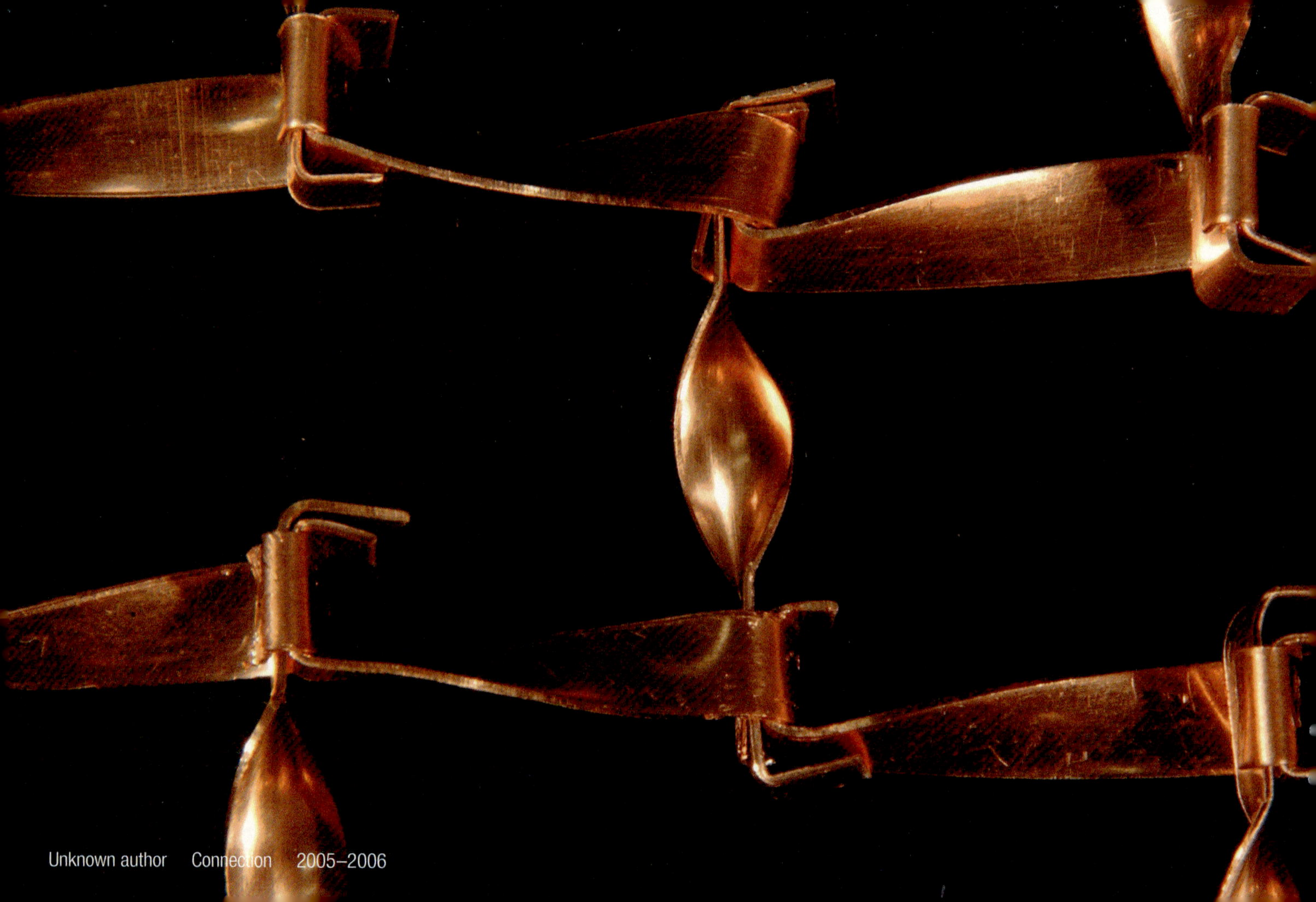

Unknown author Connection 2005–2006

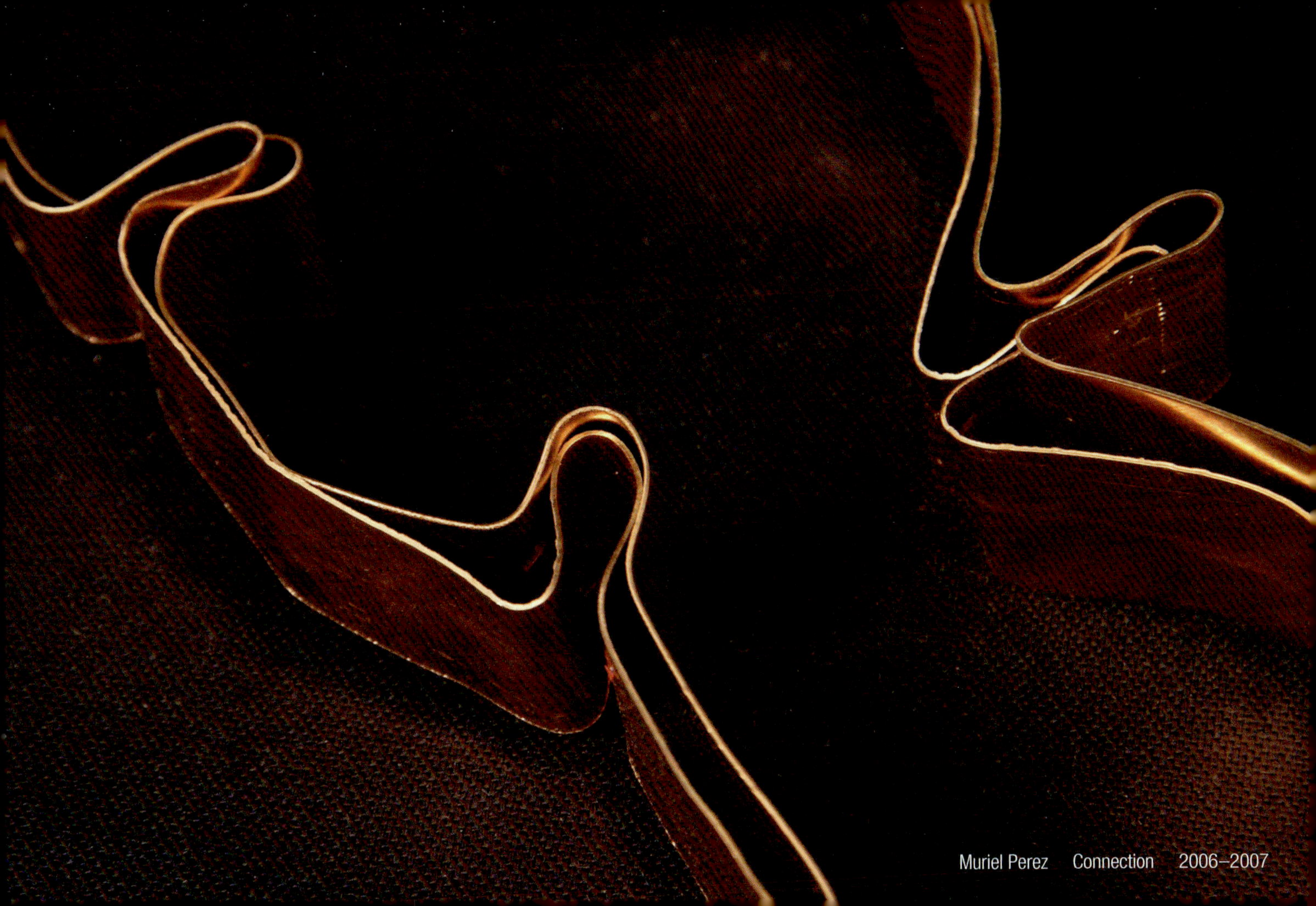

Muriel Perez Connection 2006–2007

Unknown author Connection 2005–2006

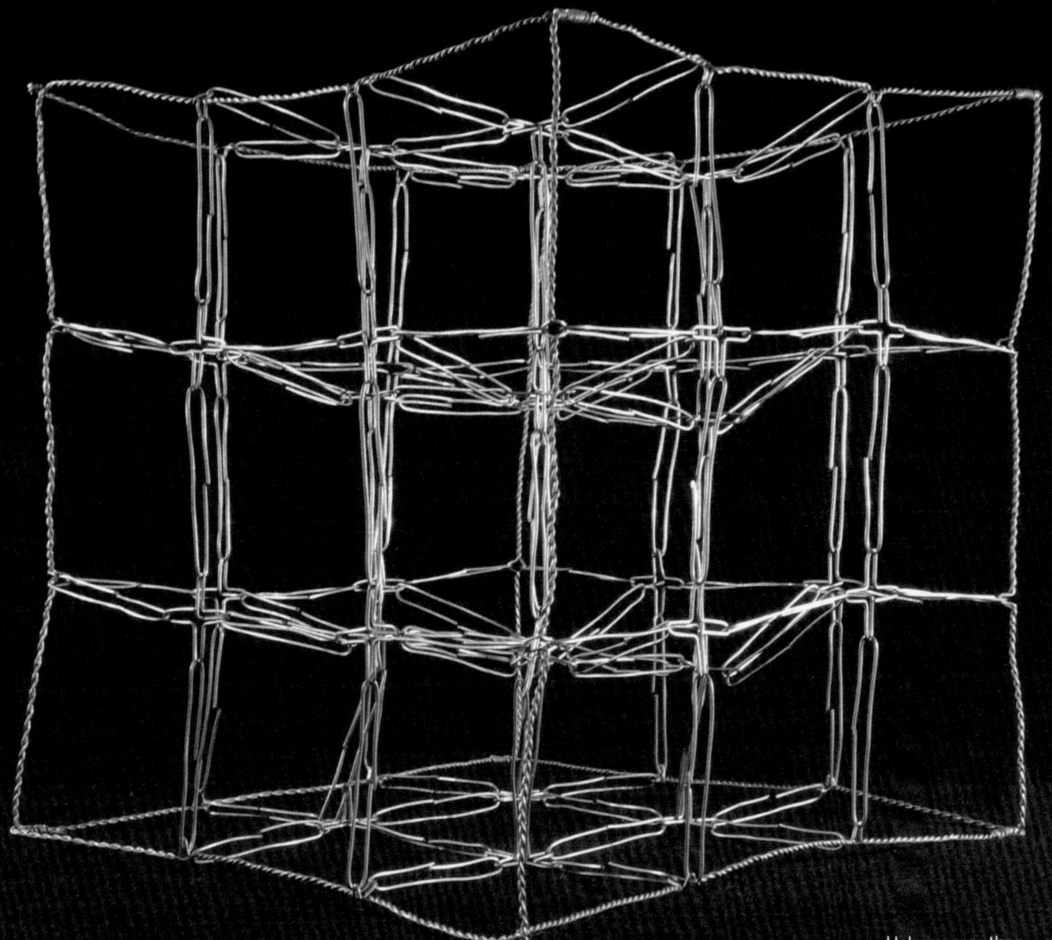

Unknown author Connection 2005–2006

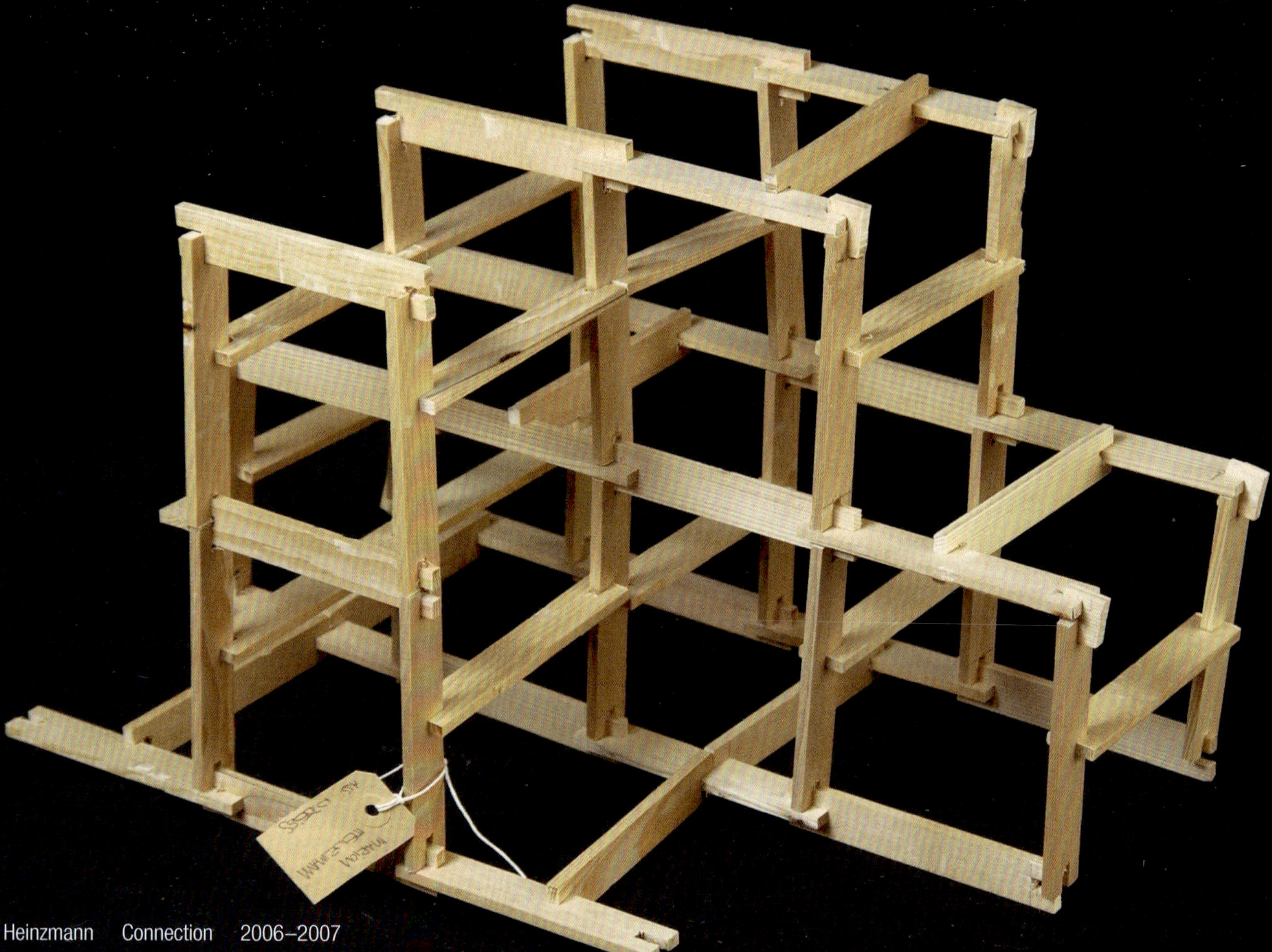

Marion Heinzmann Connection 2006–2007

Kevin Dröscher, Anna von Knobloch Support 2005–2006

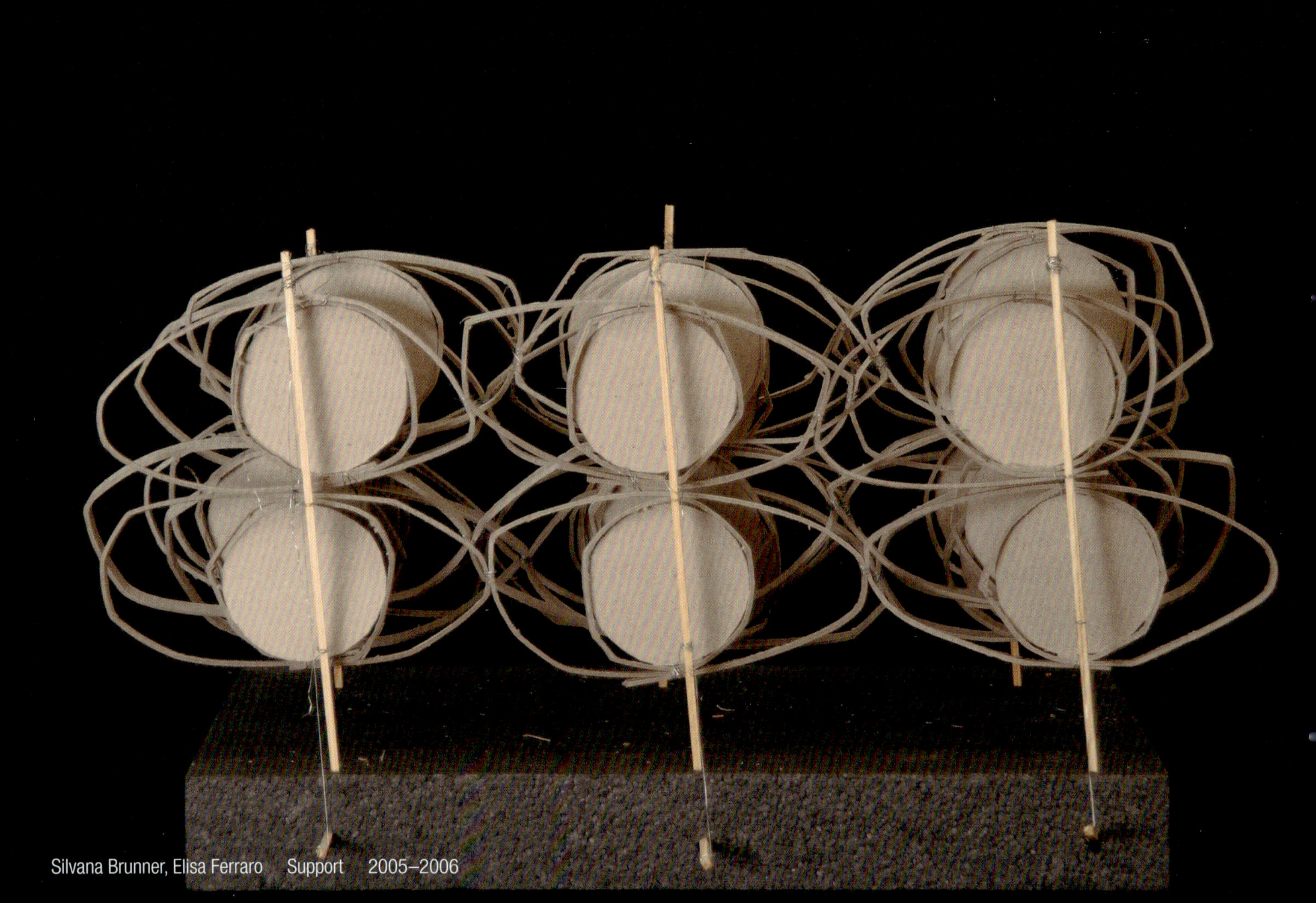

Silvana Brunner, Elisa Ferraro   Support   2005–2006

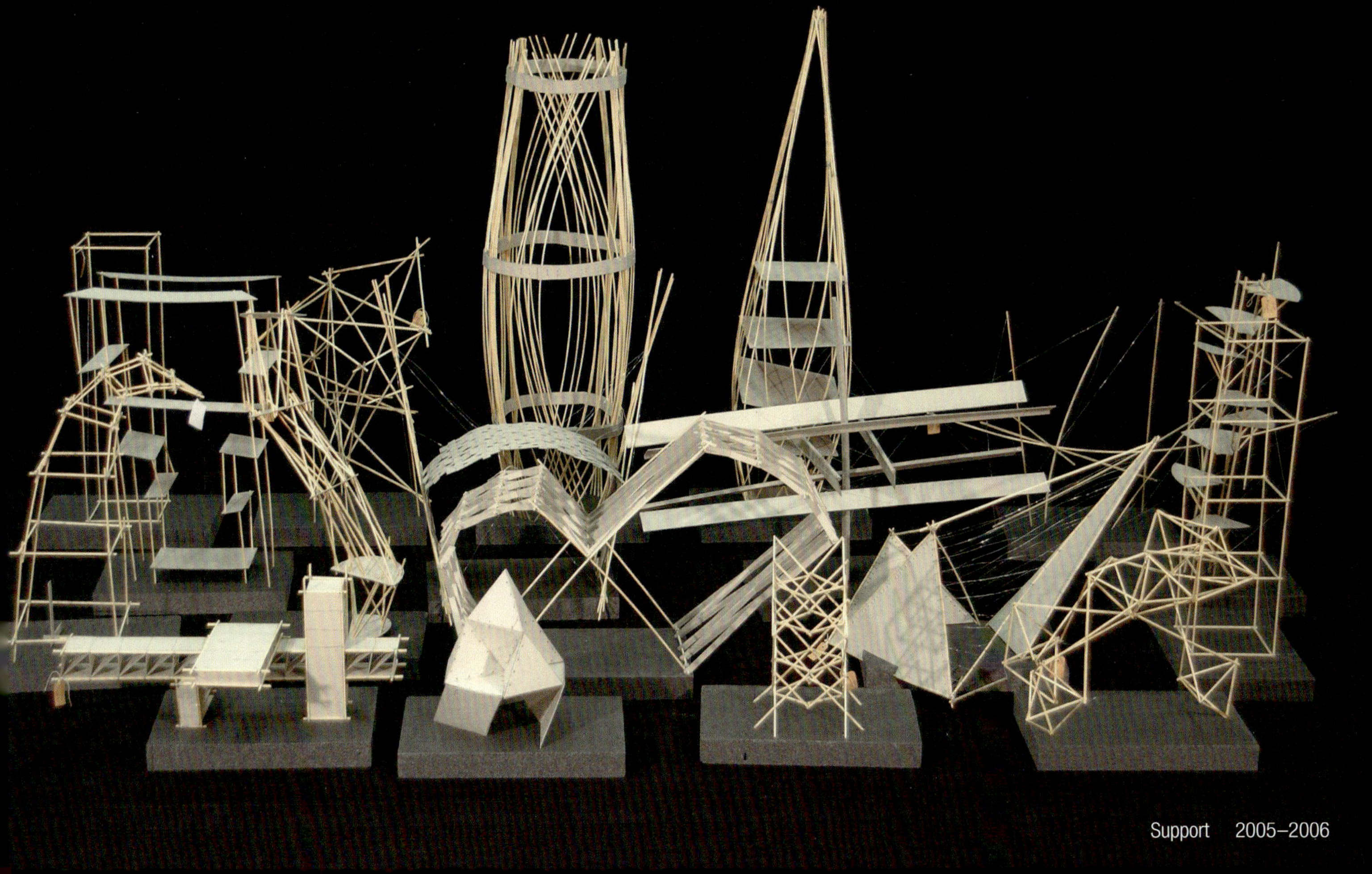

Support 2005–2006

Roman Bieri, Michael Keller Space 2005–2006

Adrian Degonda, Manuel Gander Shell 2005–2006

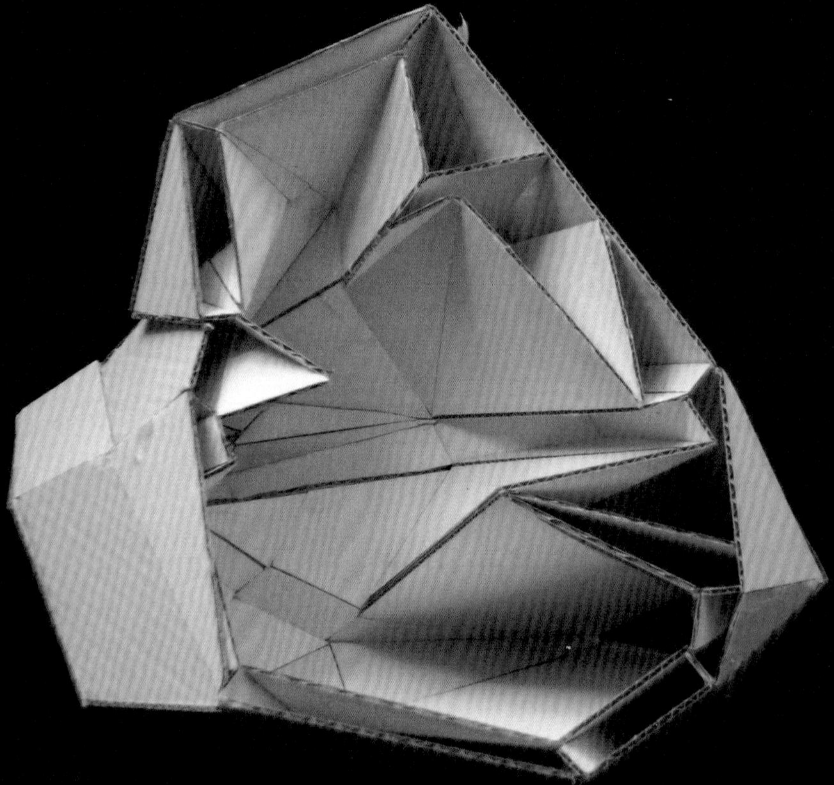

Jonas Epper, Alex Madathilparambil Shell 2005–2006

Kevin Dröscher, Anna von Knobloch Building 2005–2006

Hannah Kuby, Simona Zimmermann Constructive project 2005–2006

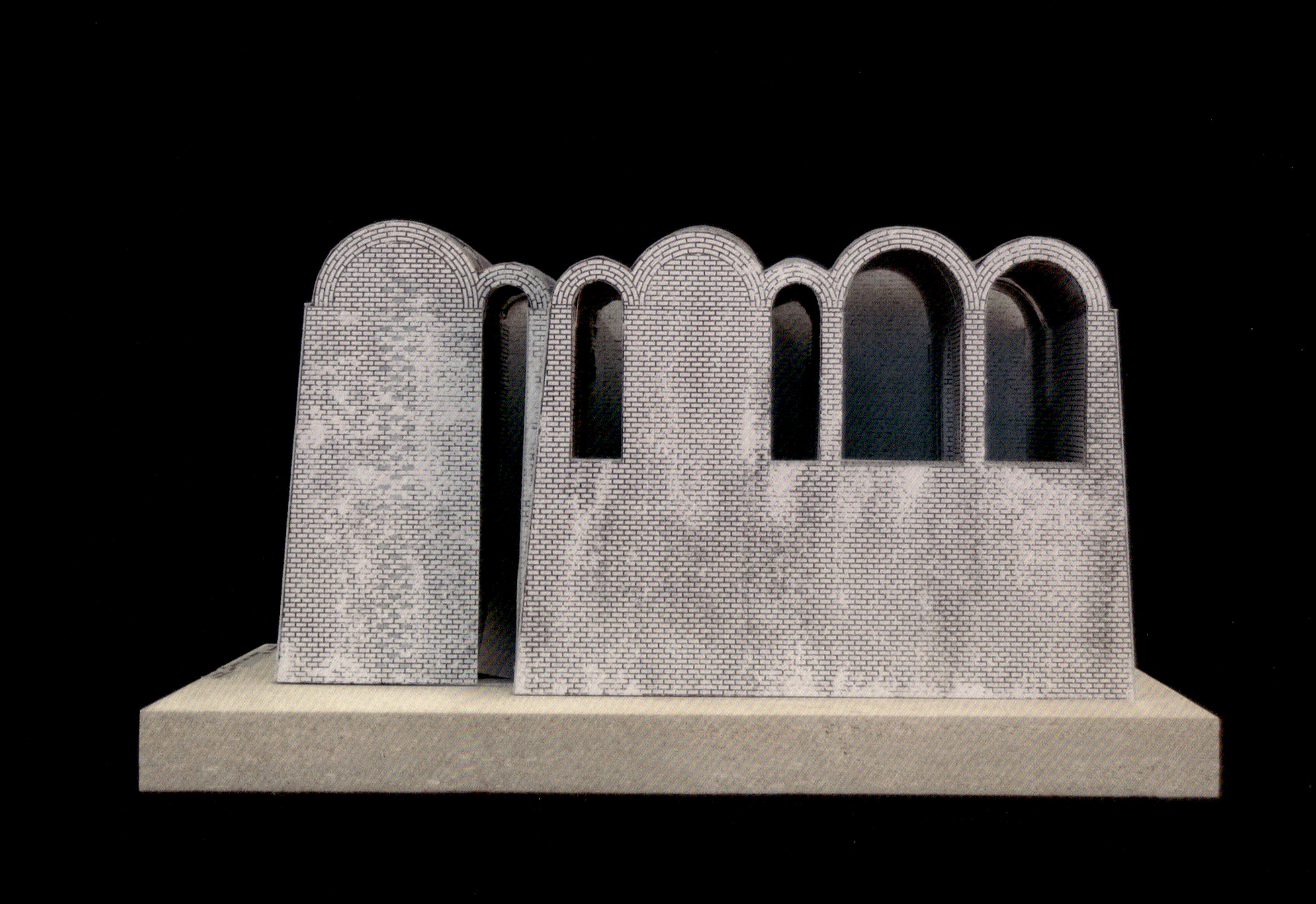

Caterina Inderbitzin, Stefanie Krautzig   Constructive project   2005–2006

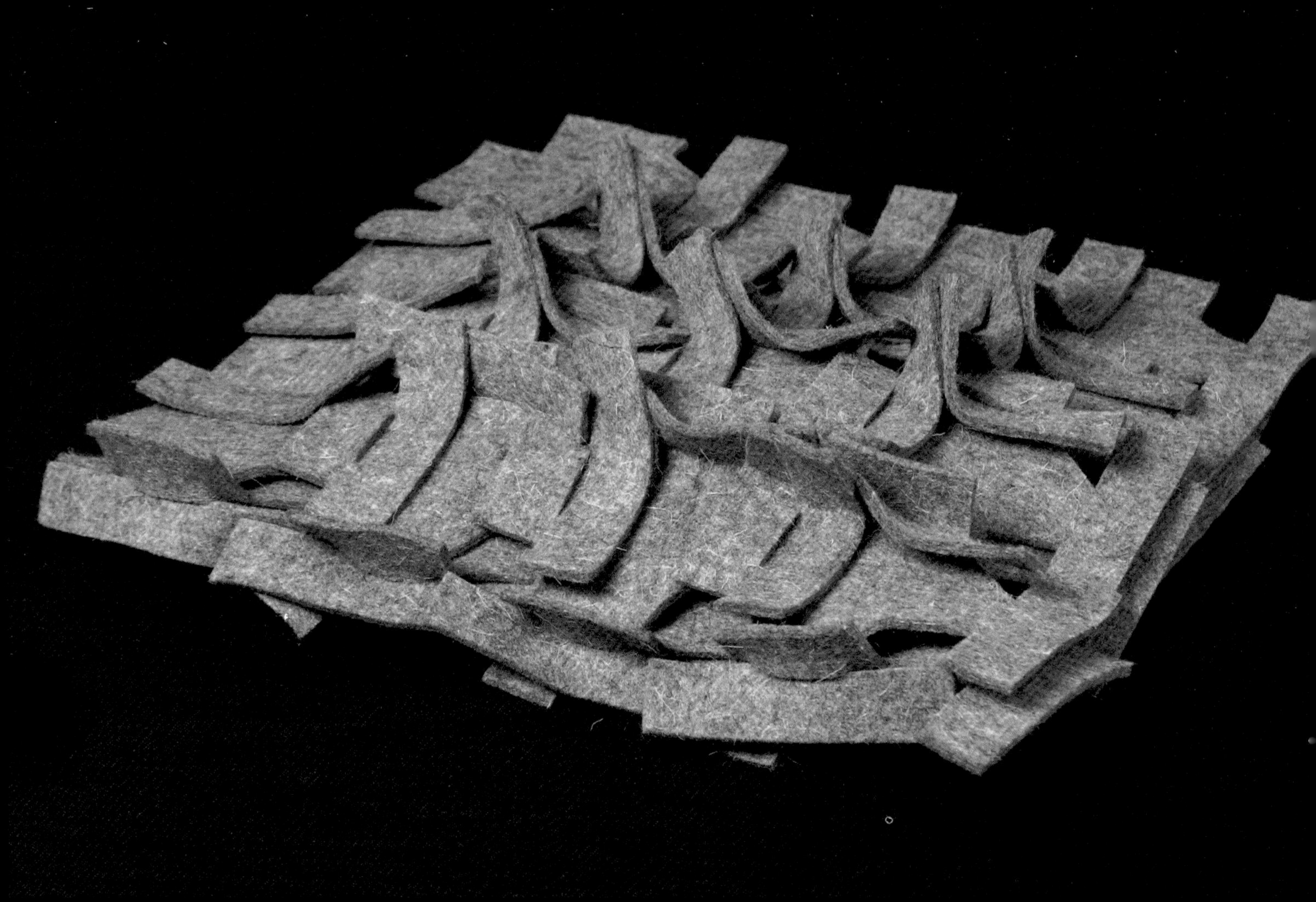

Serge Miserez Connection 2006–2007

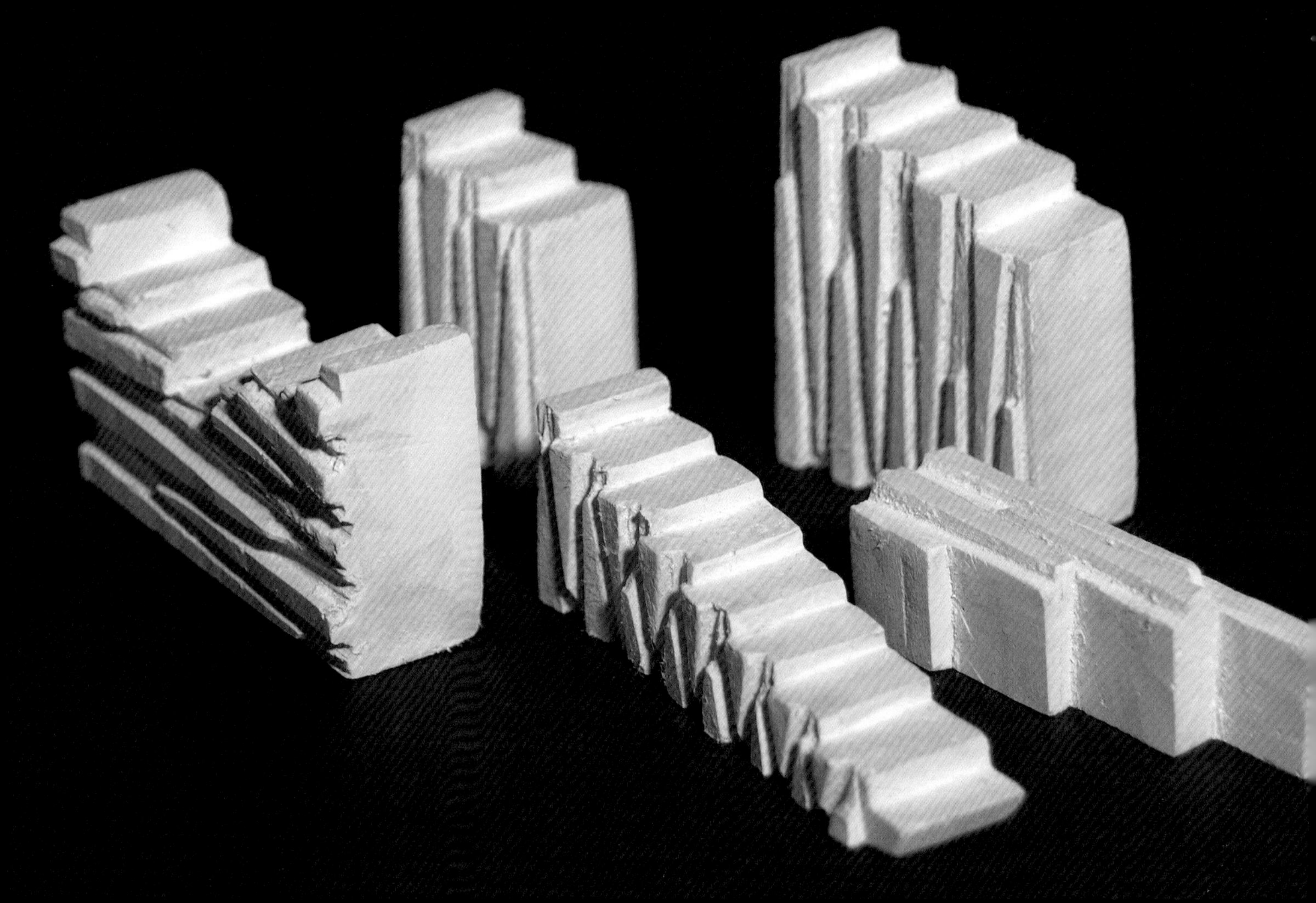

Lorenz Müller Composition 2003–2004

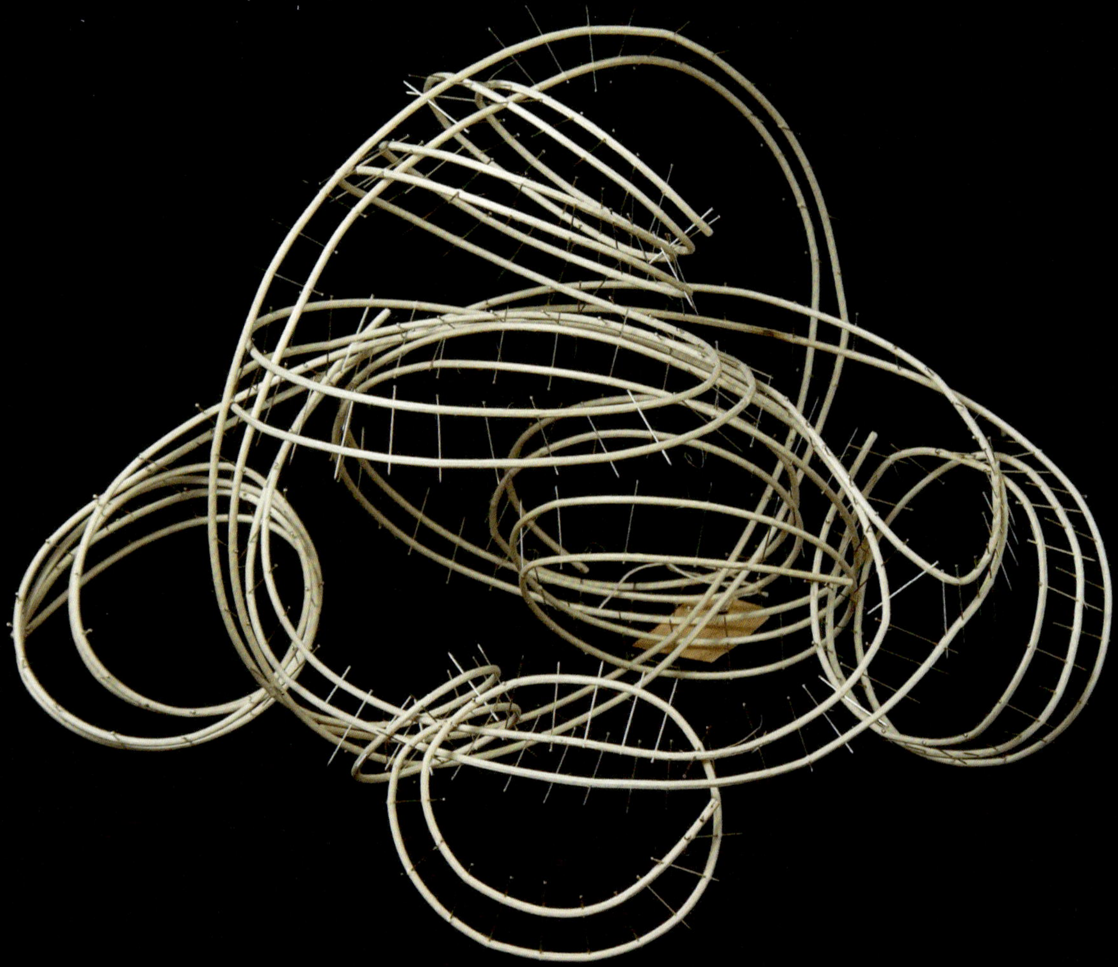

Silvana Clavuot Connection 2006–2007

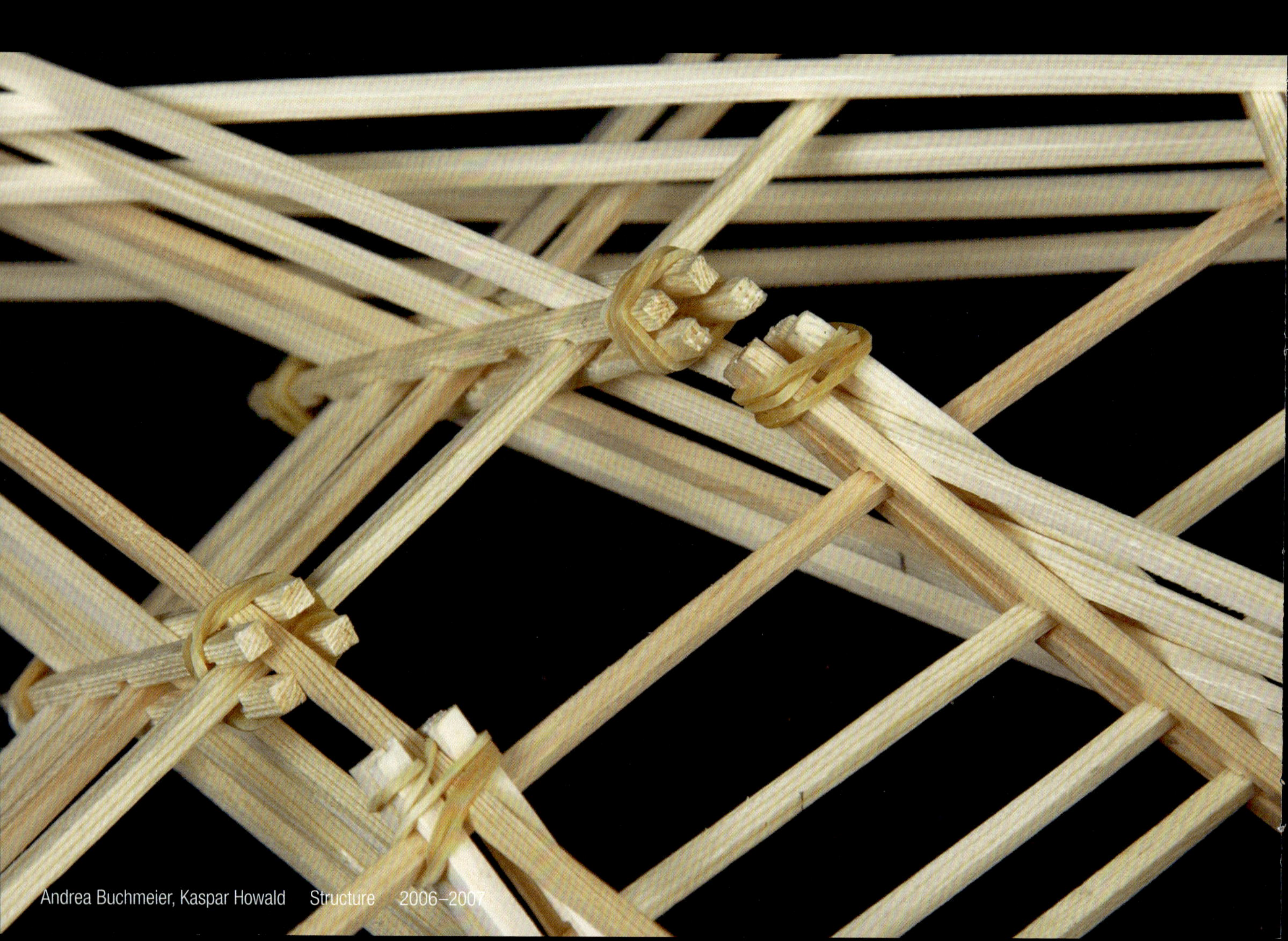

Andrea Buchmeier, Kaspar Howald Structure 2006–2007

Jérémy Stauffacher Structure 2006–2007

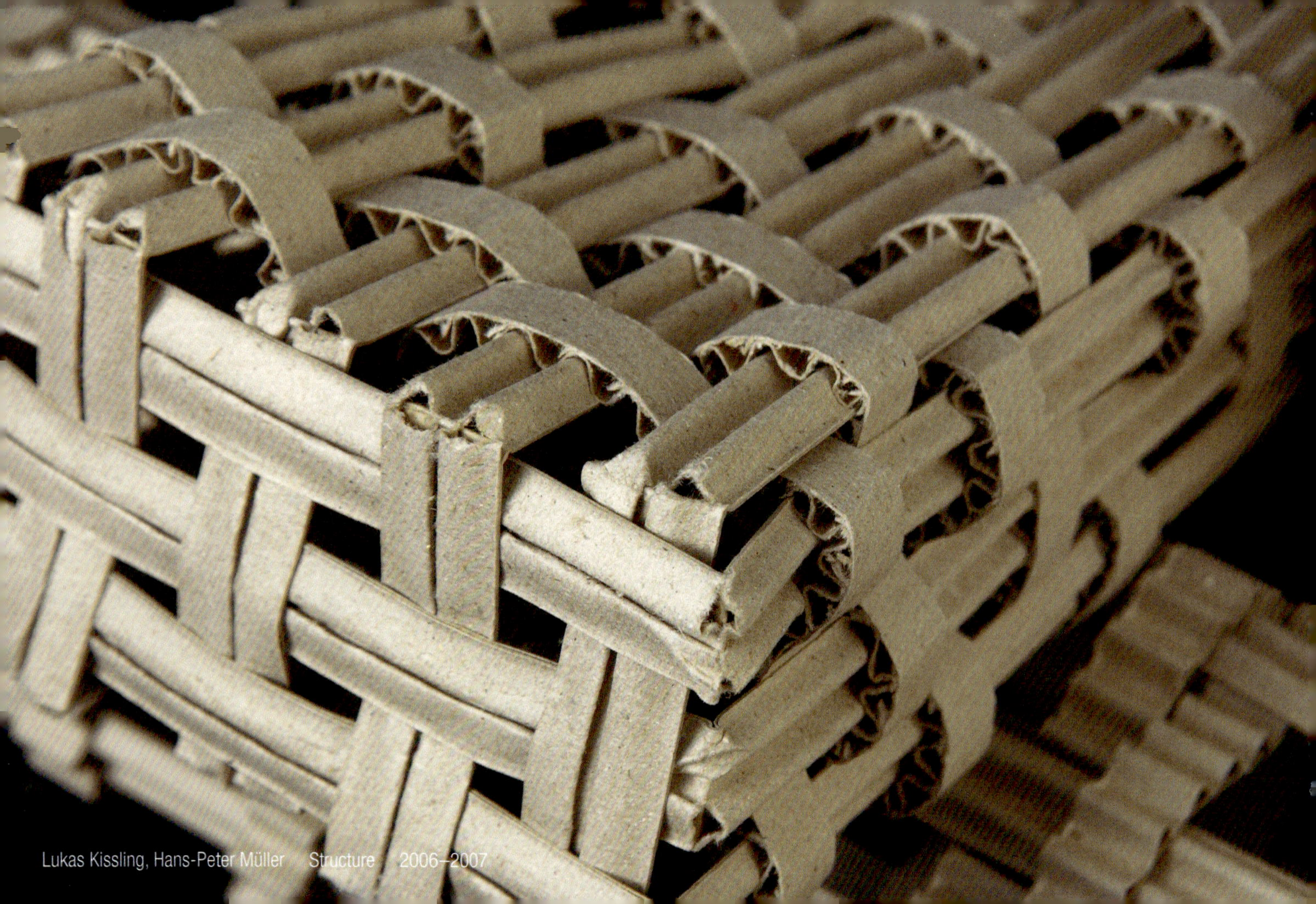

Lukas Kissling, Hans-Peter Müller Structure 2006–2007

Jennifer Karrer, Eva Lanter Structure 2006–2007

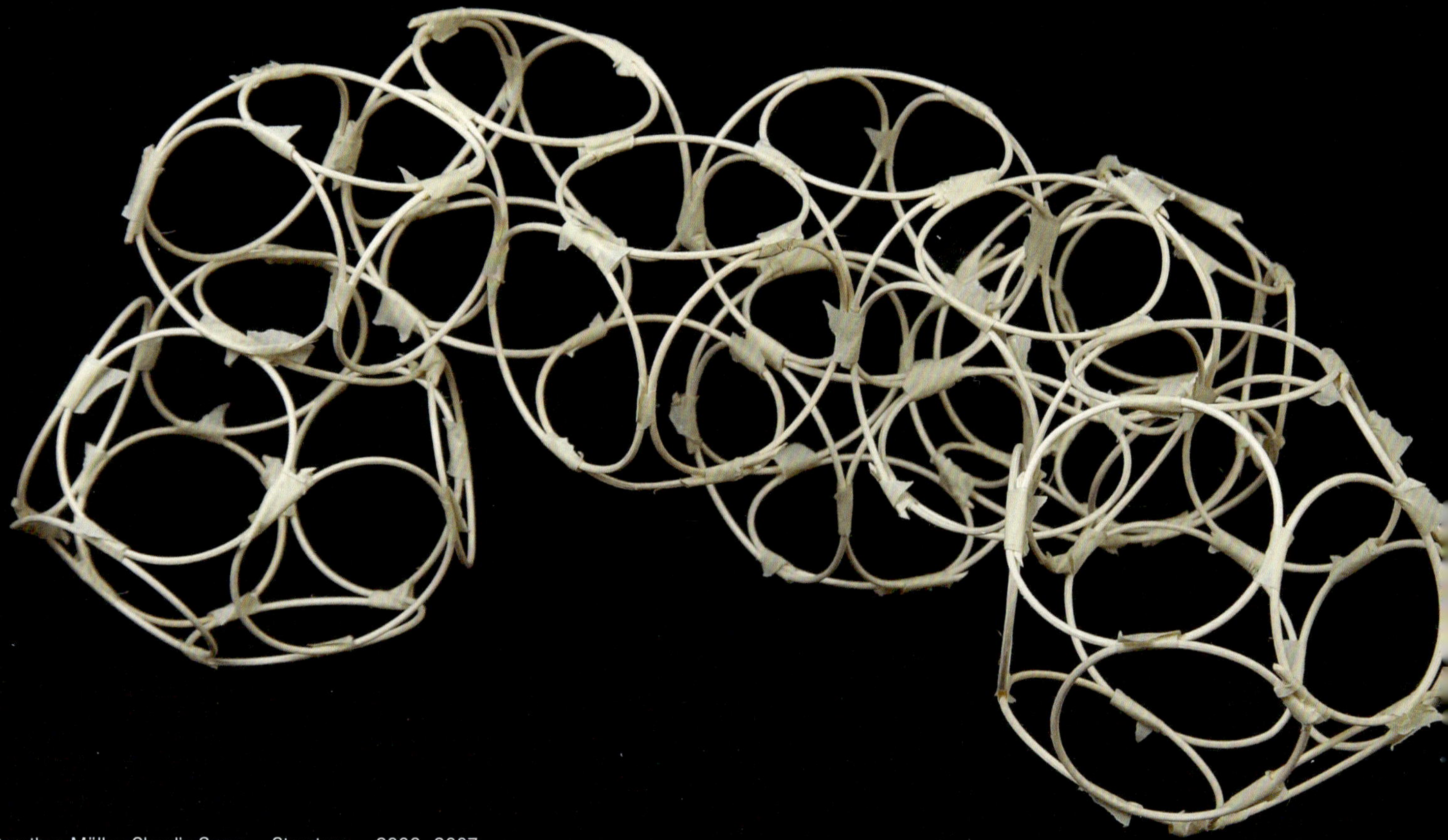

Dorothee Müller, Claudia Surer   Structure   2006–2007

Laura Burgener, Muriel Perez Space 2006–2007

Laura Burgener, Muriel Perez Shell 2006–2007

Nathanael Müller, Stephan Pfeiffer Building 2006–2007

Jan Dlabac, Serge Miserez Building 2006–2007

Jan Dlabac, Serge Miserez   Building   2006–2007

Bianca Kummer, Micha Weber Building 2006–2007

Michel Frei, Stephie Pfenninger Building 2006–2007

Mischa Jäggi, Elina Müller Building 2006–2007

Thomas Hungerbühler, Matthias Stücheli Constructive project 2004–2005

Oliver Muff, David Späh Building 2006–2007

Constructive project 1997–1998

Daniel Coll y Capdevila Tomography 1997–1998

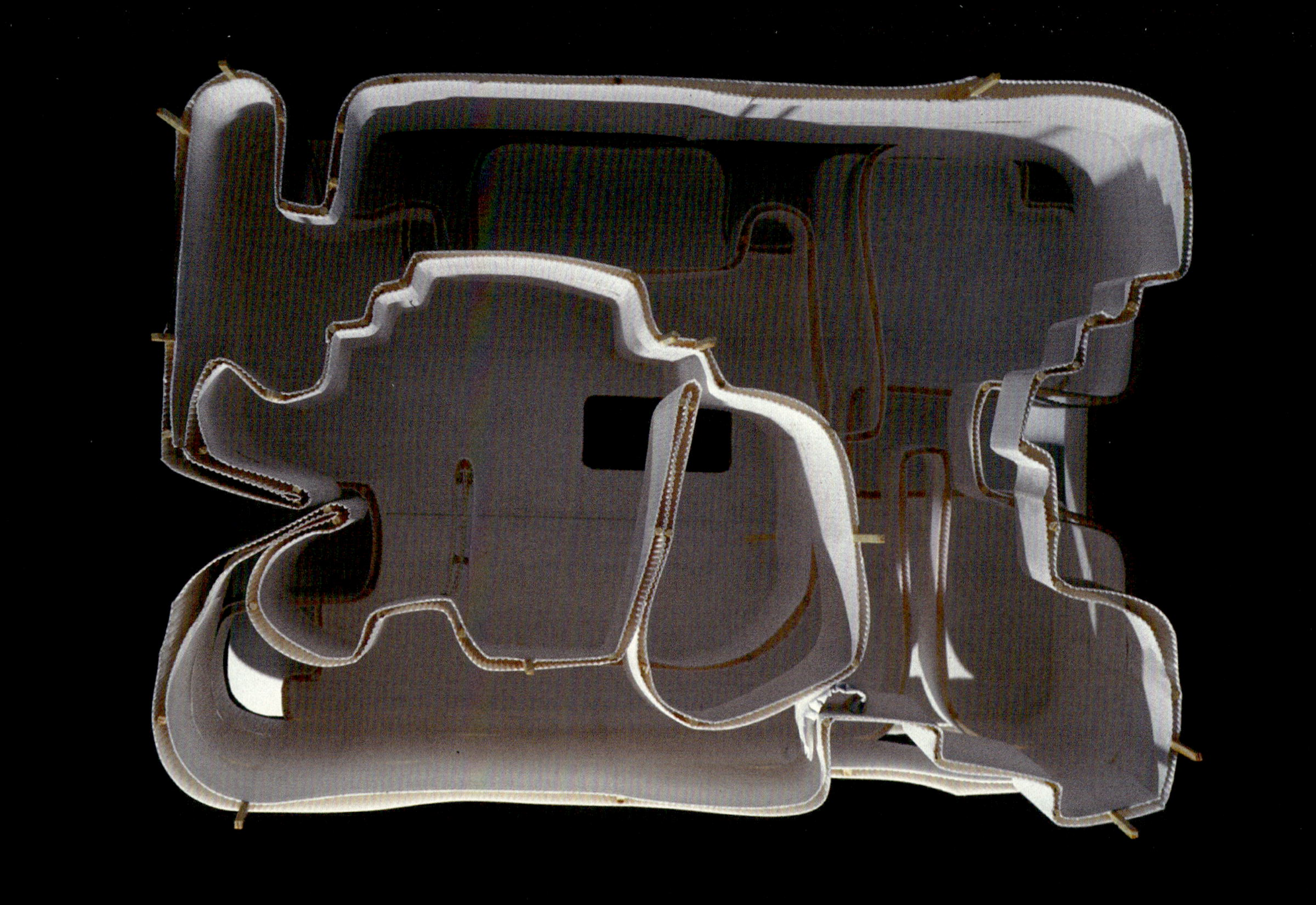

Damian Walliser Glove 1998–1999

Marc Bühler Glove 1998–1999

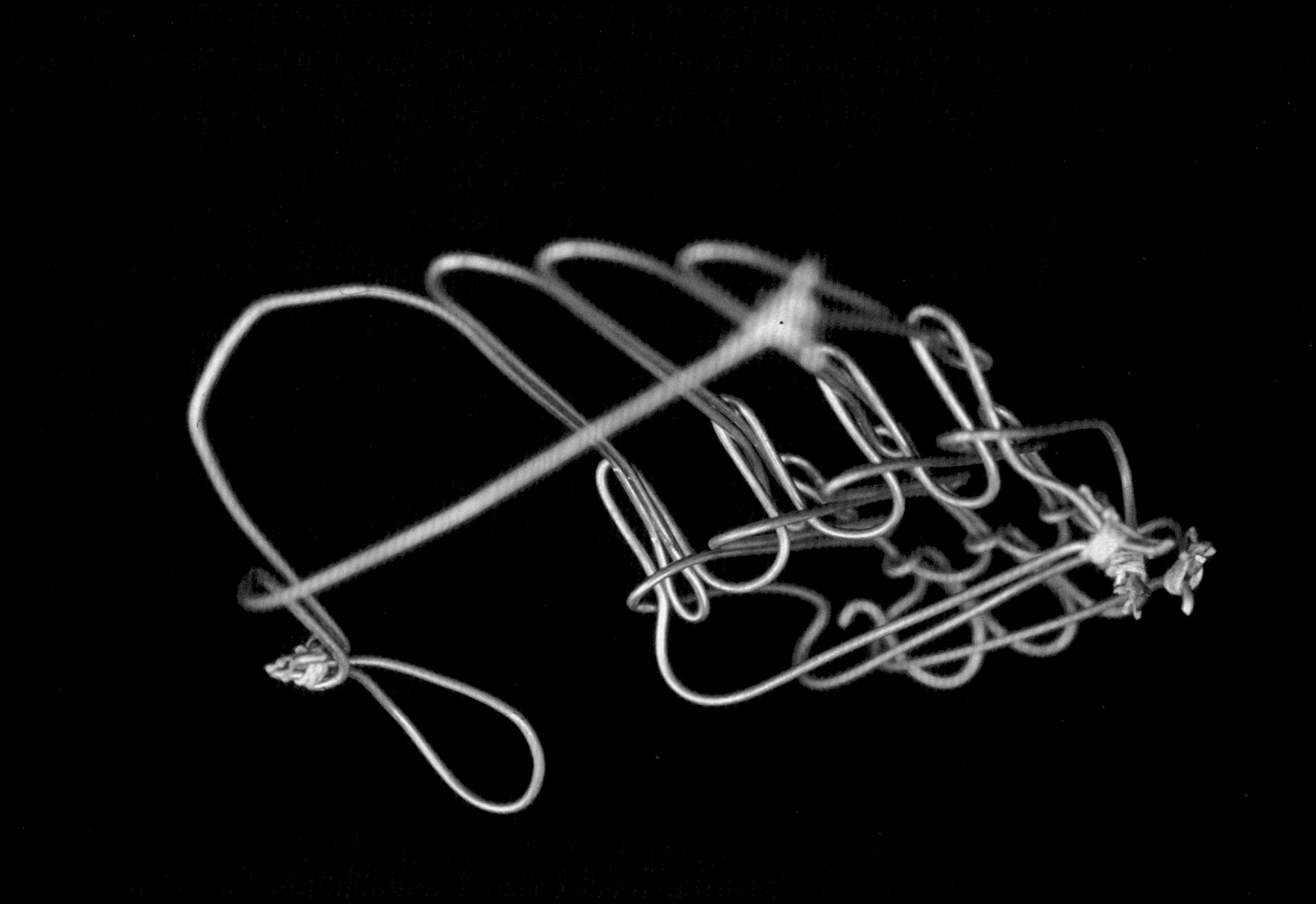

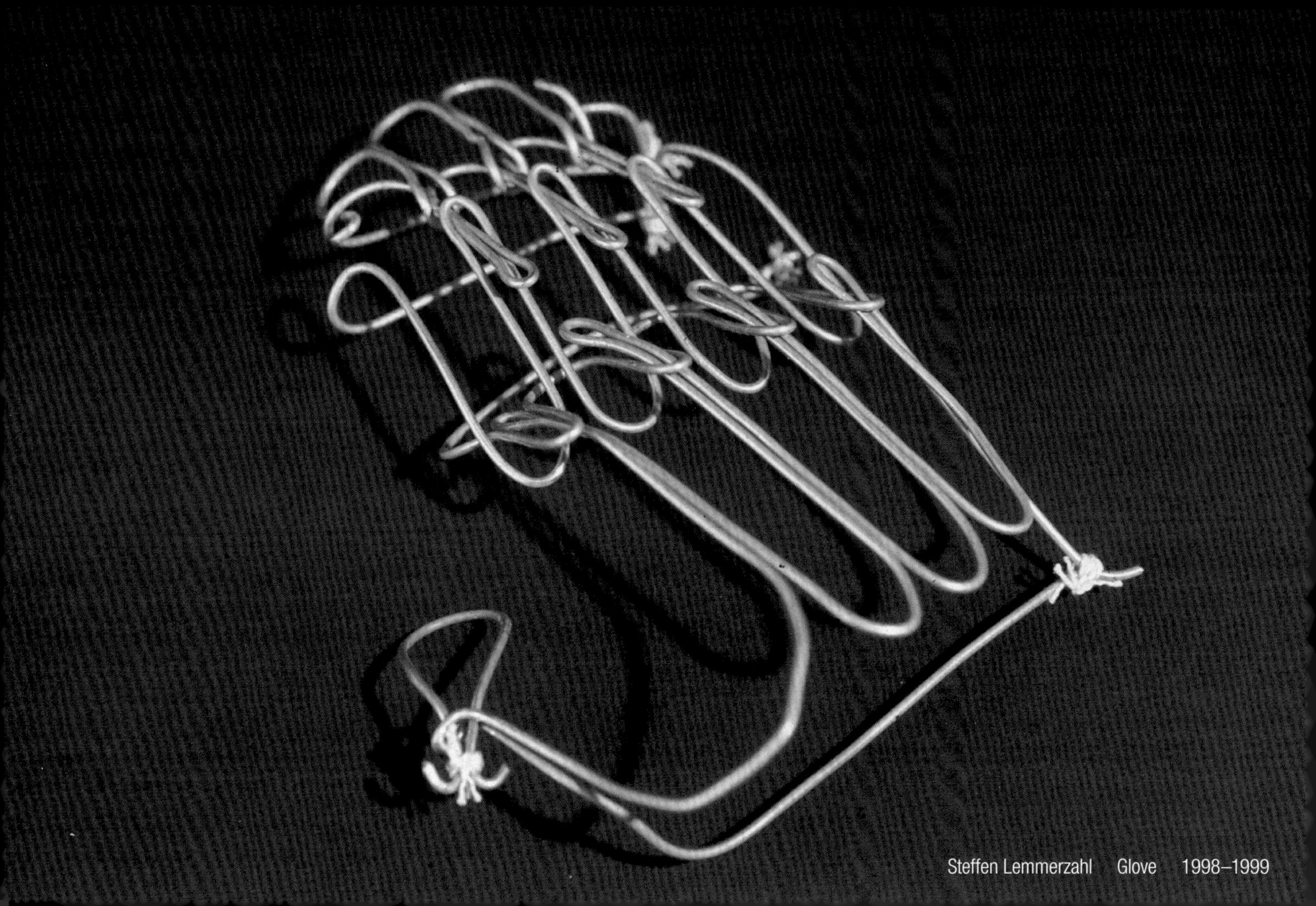

Steffen Lemmerzahl Glove 1998–1999

Andrea Buchmeier, Kaspar Howald Building 2006–2007

Fund Räumling 1997–1998

Heinz Rempfler   Räumling   1997–1998

Isabella Aurich Räumling 1997–1998

Isabella Aurich Räumling 1997–1998

Isabella Aurich Räumling 1997–1998

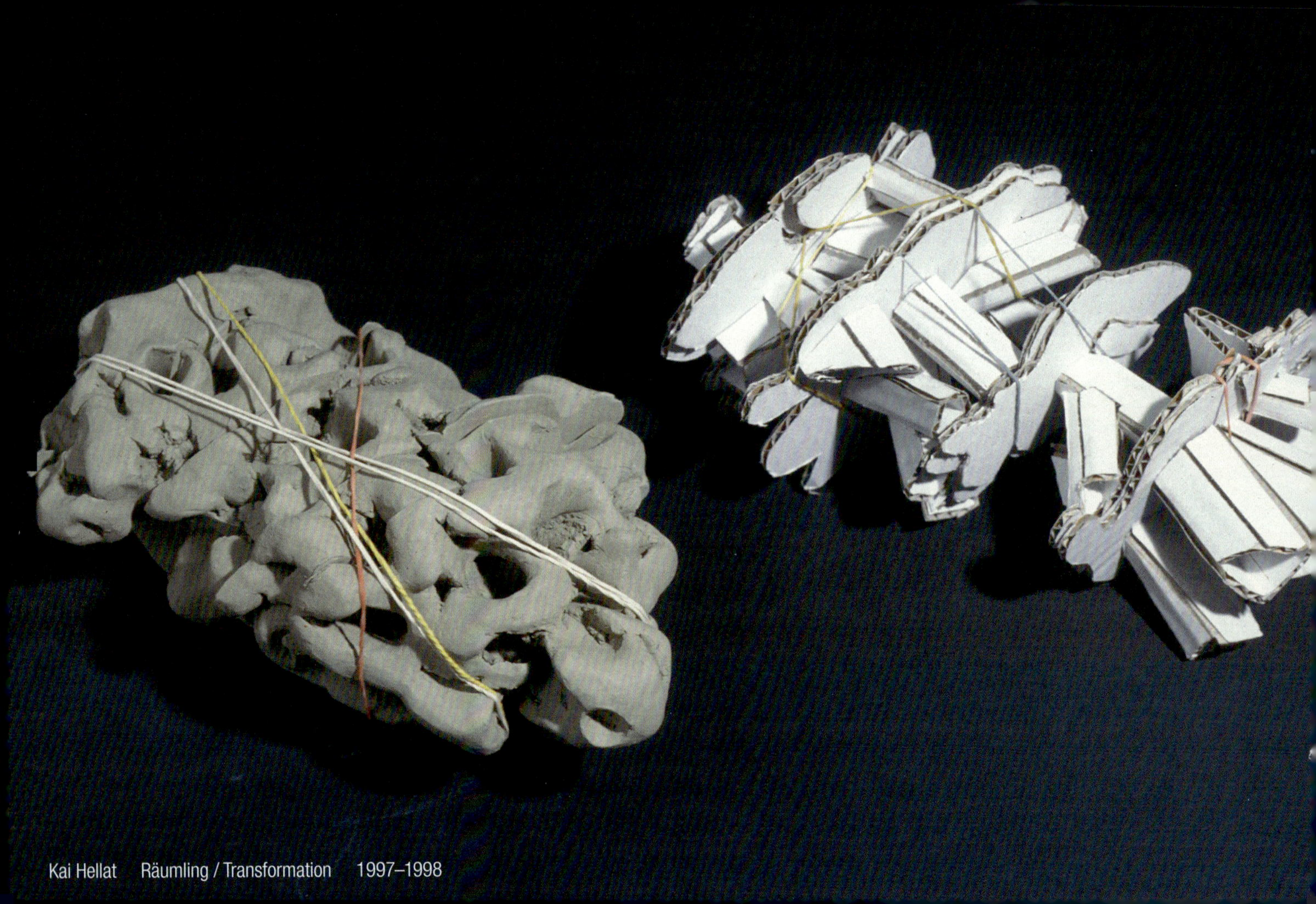

Kai Hellat Räumling / Transformation 1997–1998

Lawrence Quiblier   Räumling / Transformation   1997–1998

Christian Mueller Tomography 1997–1998

Alexander Schaerer, Martien Schoep Composition 1997–1998

Aleksandar Vucenovic Composition 1997–1998

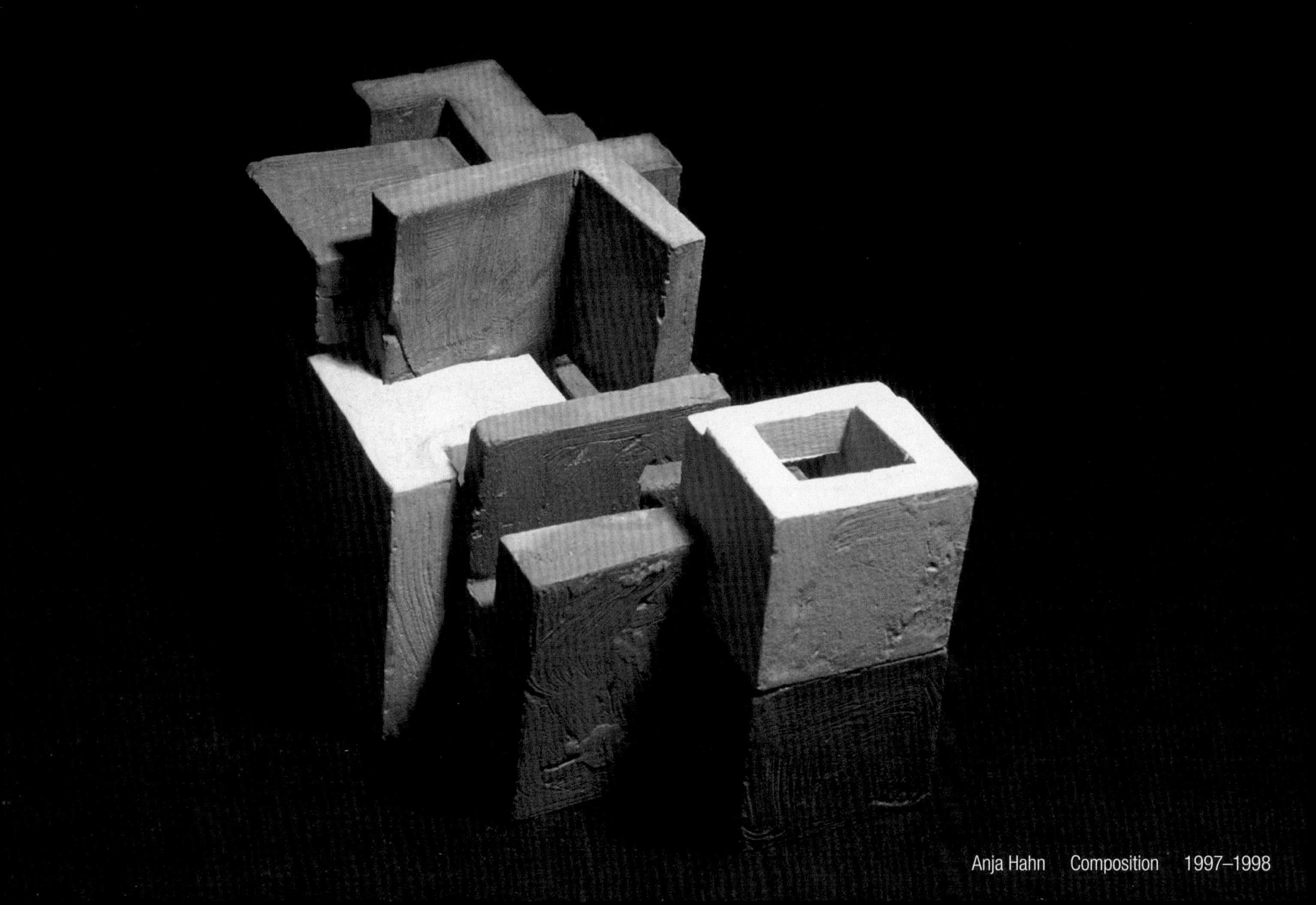

Anja Hahn Composition 1997–1998

Unknown author Composition 1997–1998

Florian Eberle, Benedikt Gruetter   Composition   1997–1998

Christiane Felber Composition 1997–1998

Claudia Vosti Composition 1997–1998

Dominique Wyttenbach   Composition   1997–1998

Philipp Günther Composition 1997–1998

Hendrik David, Julian Schramek   Composition   1997–1998

Raphael Haefeli, Jürg Keller Composition 1997–1998

Michel Lazecki, Christof Lippuner   Composition   1997–1998

Rebecca Lehmann Composition 1997–1998

Ariel Koechlin, Nicolas Rudin   Constructive project   2005–2006

Mischa Jäggi, Elina Müller Building 2006–2007

Simon Hodel, Thomas Kissling   Building   2005–2006

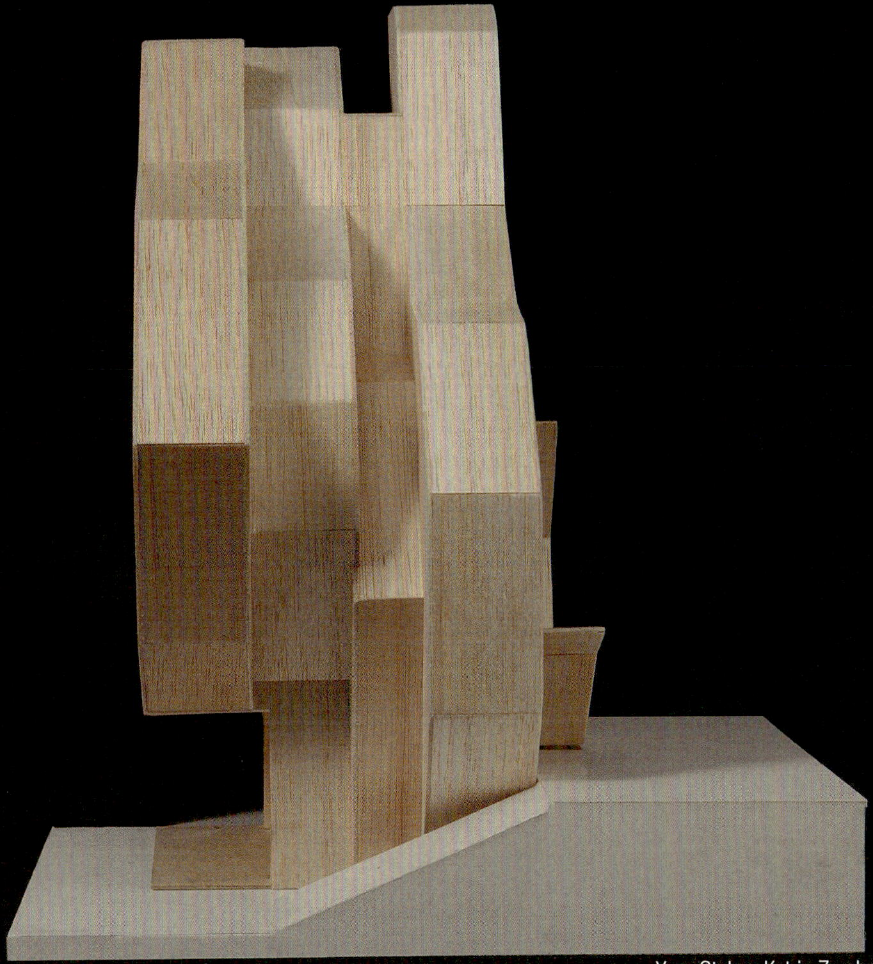

Yves Stuber, Katrin Zumbrunnen Building 2006–2007

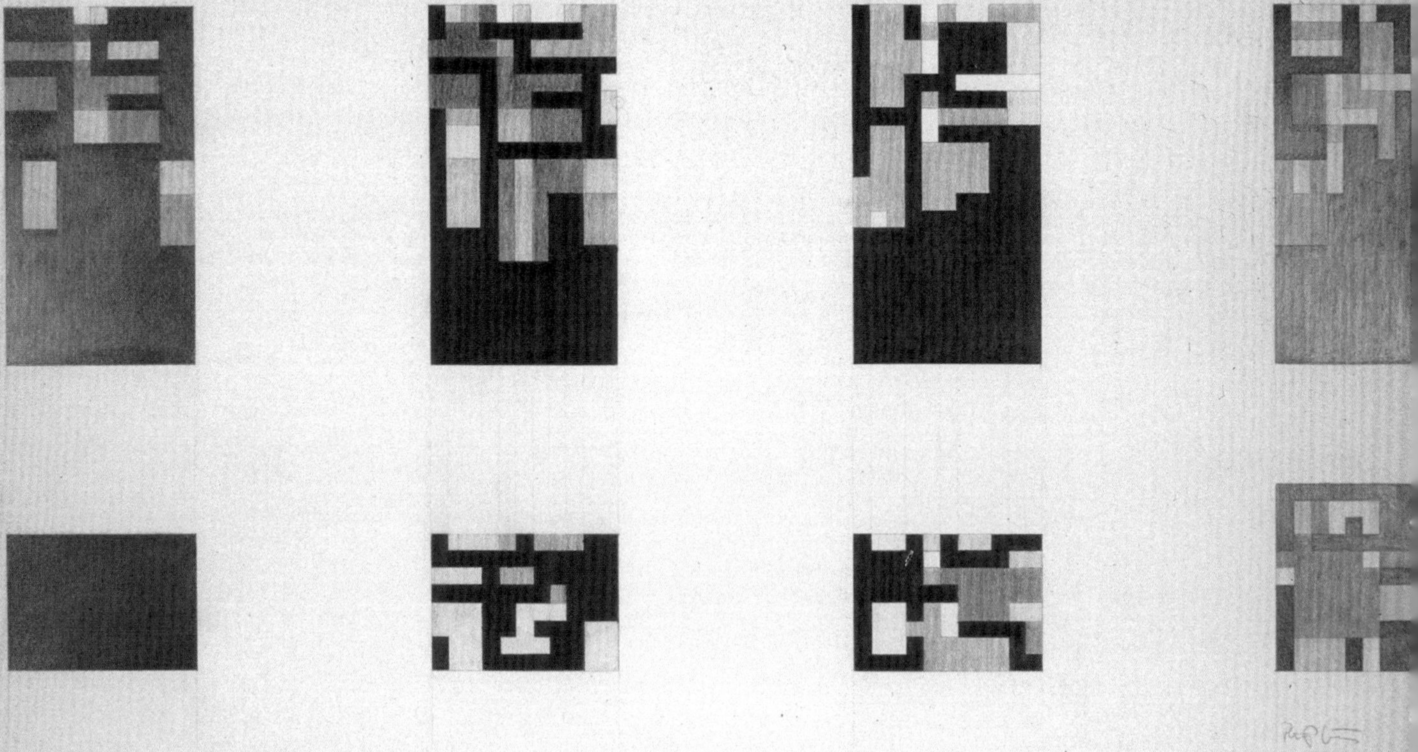

Philip König Tomography 1998–1999

Thomas Juon, Nina Täschler   Constructive project   2004–2005

Bettine Volk Composition 1998–1999

Dieter Grab   Composition   1998–1999

Florian Jennewein Composition 1998–1999

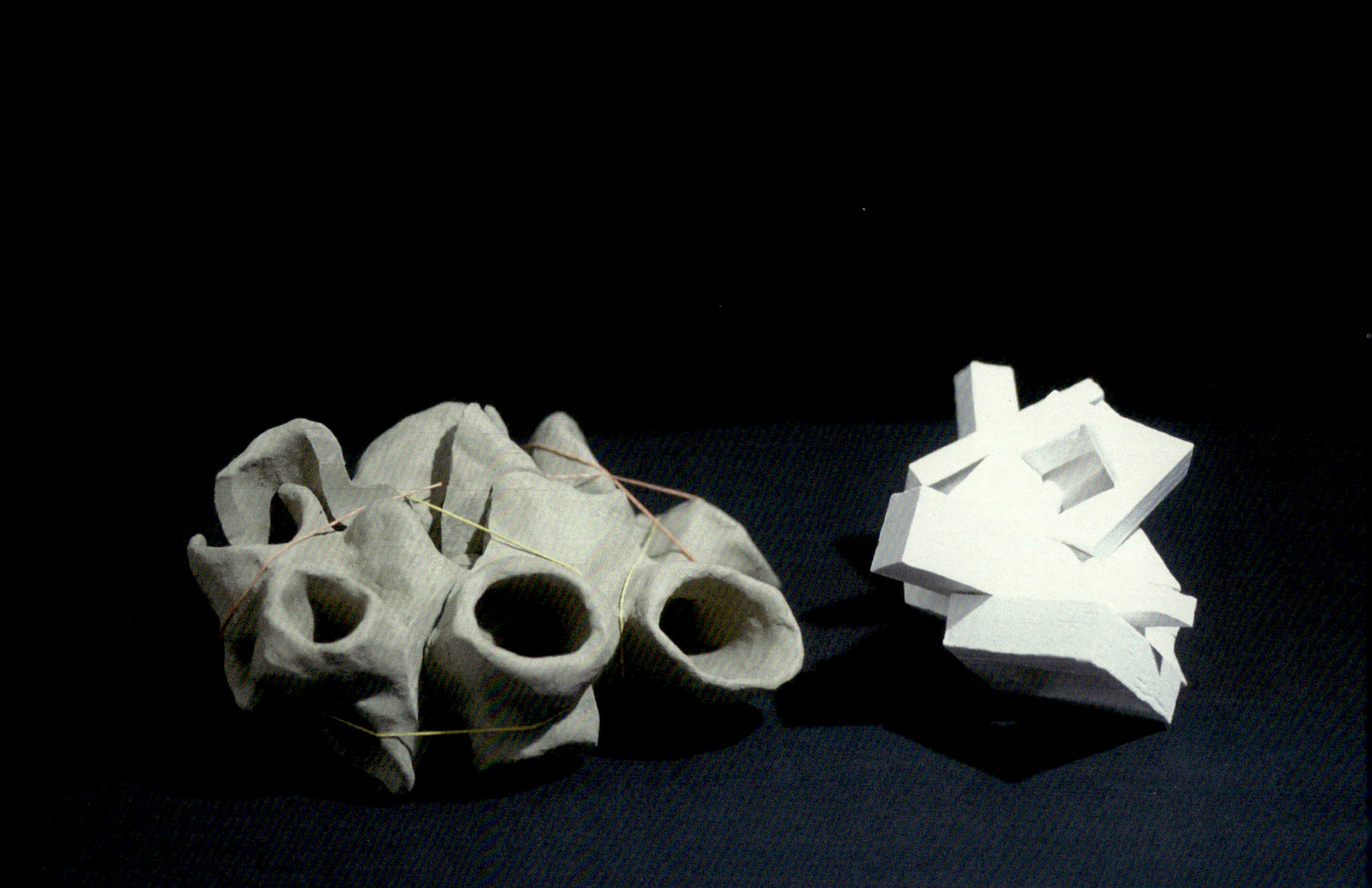

Nic Wallimann   Räumling / Composition   1998–1999

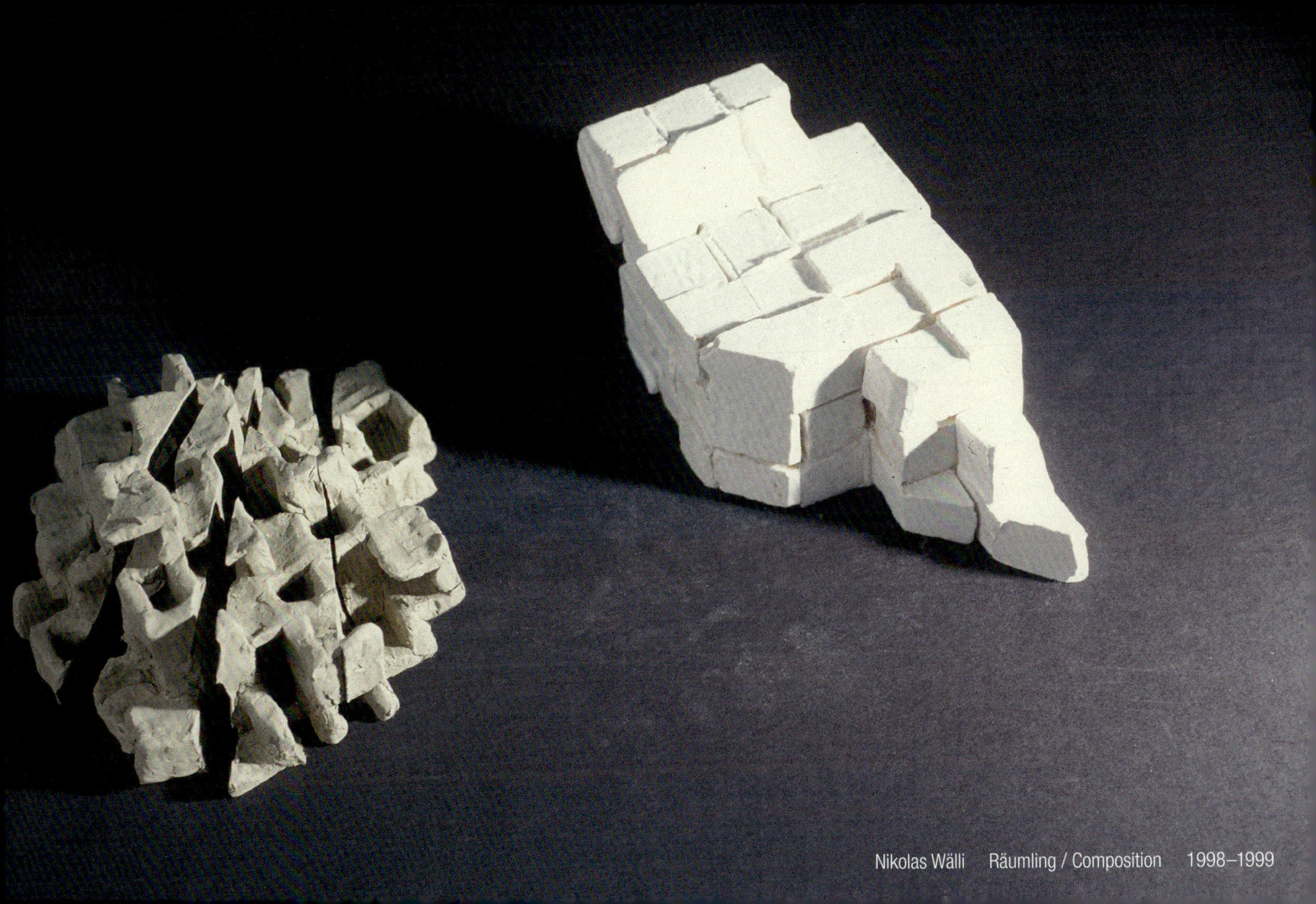

Nikolas Wälli Räumling / Composition 1998–1999

Kathrin Troxler Composition 1998–1999

Philip König Composition 1998–1999

Alexander Dick Transformation 1999–2000

Hendrik David, Julian Schramek Composition 1997–1998

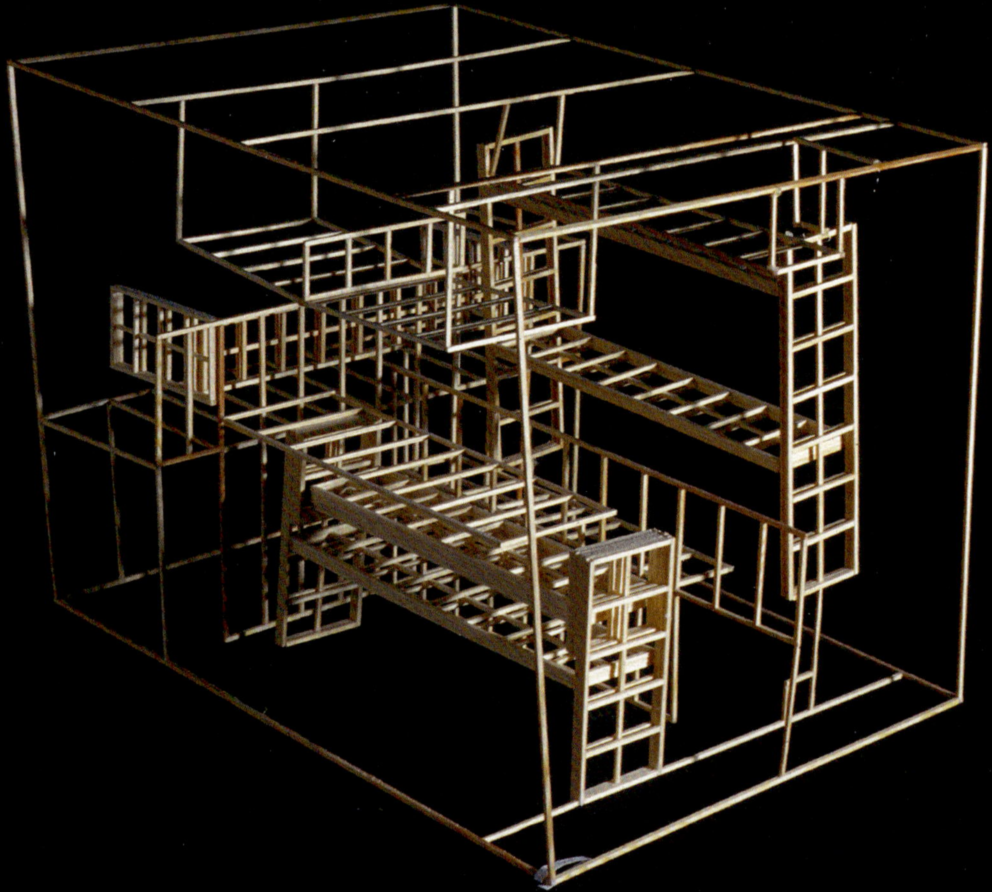

Kathrin Hofmann, Flavian Lekkas   Structure   1998-

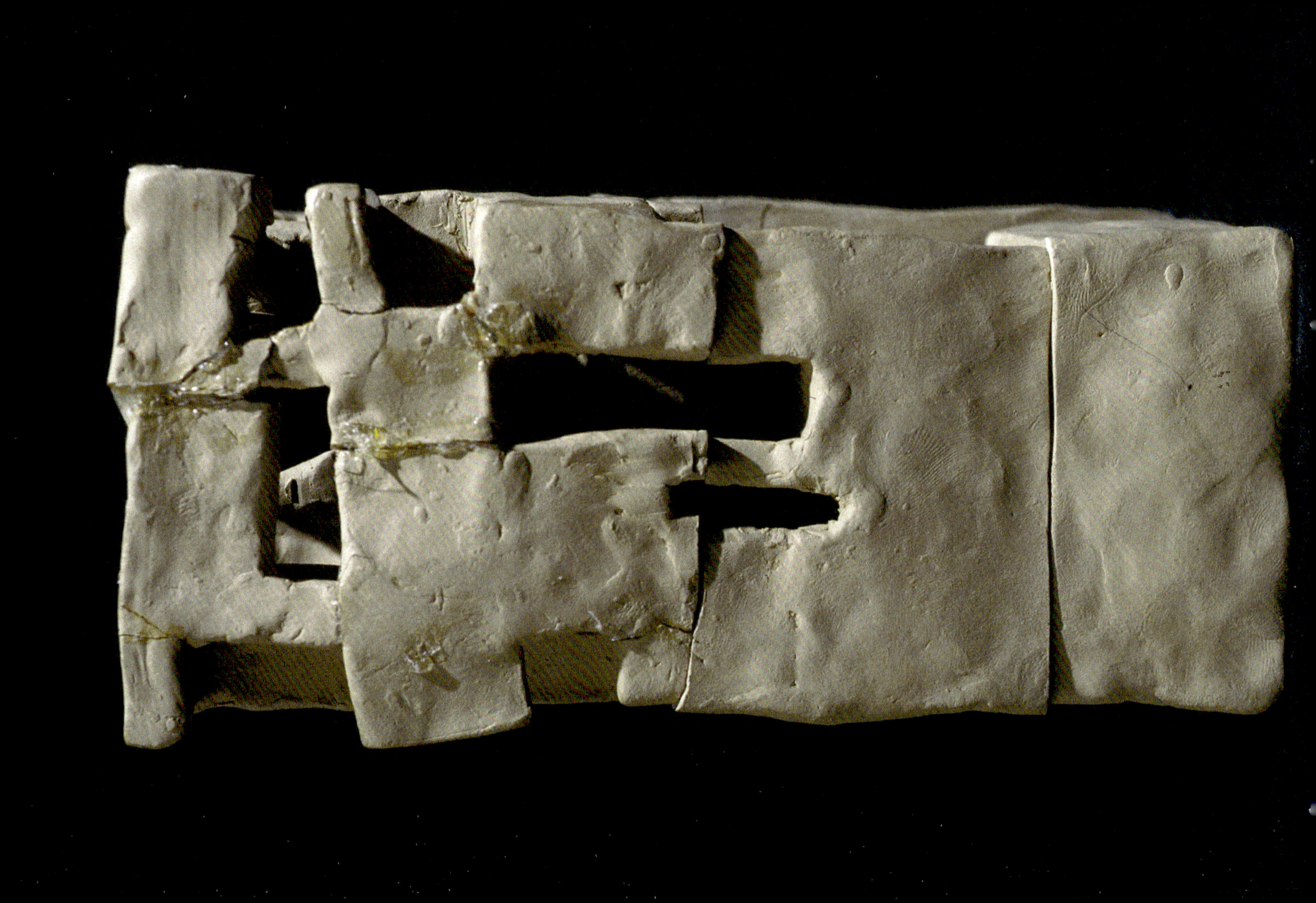

Philip König Räumling 1998–1999

Michael Broggi Glove 1999–2000

Oliver Kaufmann Glove 1999–2000

Désirée Schön Transformation 1999–2000

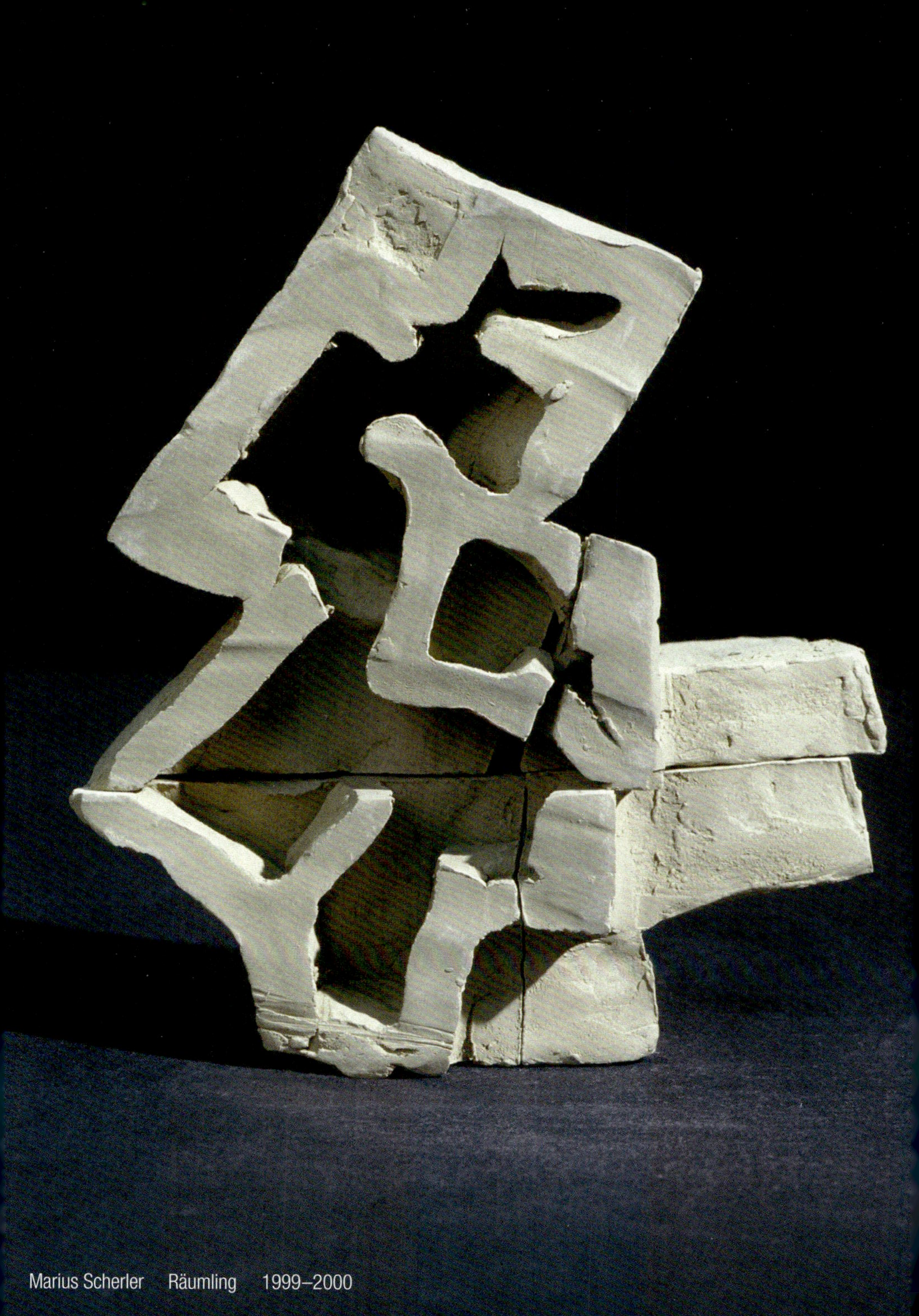

Marius Scherler Räumling 1999–2000

Florian Jennewein   Räumling   1999–2000

Florian Jennewein Transformation 1999–2000

Helen Dörflinger Räumling 1999–2000

Philip König   Räumling   1999–2000

Philip König Transformation 1999–2000

Caspar Hirzel, Hermann Knoblauch Tectonics 1999–2000

Tanja Hirsig, Thomas Wegener   Tectonics   1999–2000

Daniela Boner, Silvia Schneider   Tectonics   1999–2000

Karina Hüssner, Anna-Katharina Weber Tectonics 1999–2000

Fabienne Hoelzel, Salome Kuratli Composition 1999–2000

Patrick Maisano, Beatrice Roth   Tectonics   1999–2000

Patrick Maisano, Beatrice Roth Composition 1999–2000

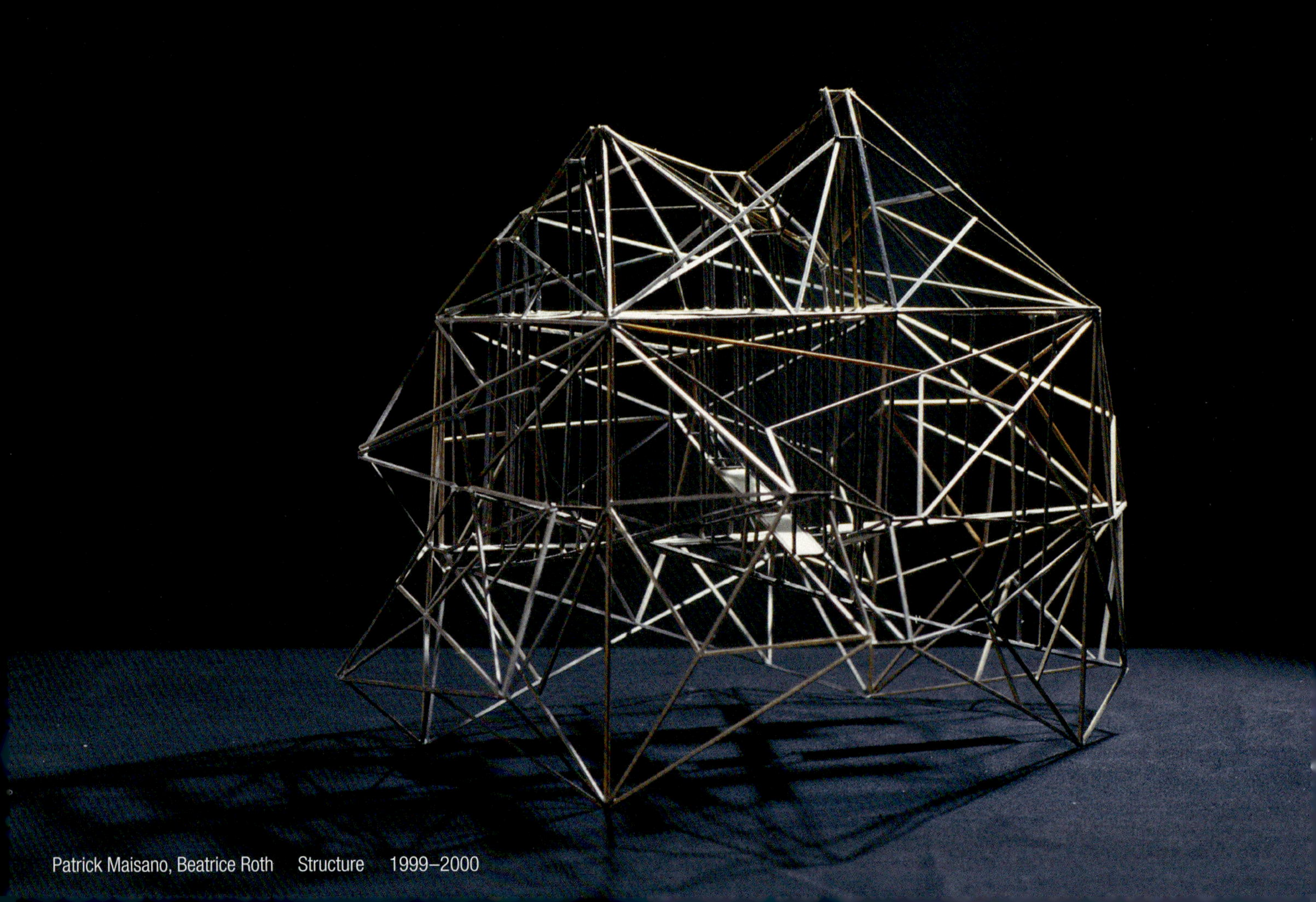

Patrick Maisano, Beatrice Roth Structure 1999–2000

Sandra Hons, Claudia Loewe Composition 1999–2000

Nathalie von Känel, Rebecca Taraborrelli Composition 1999–2000

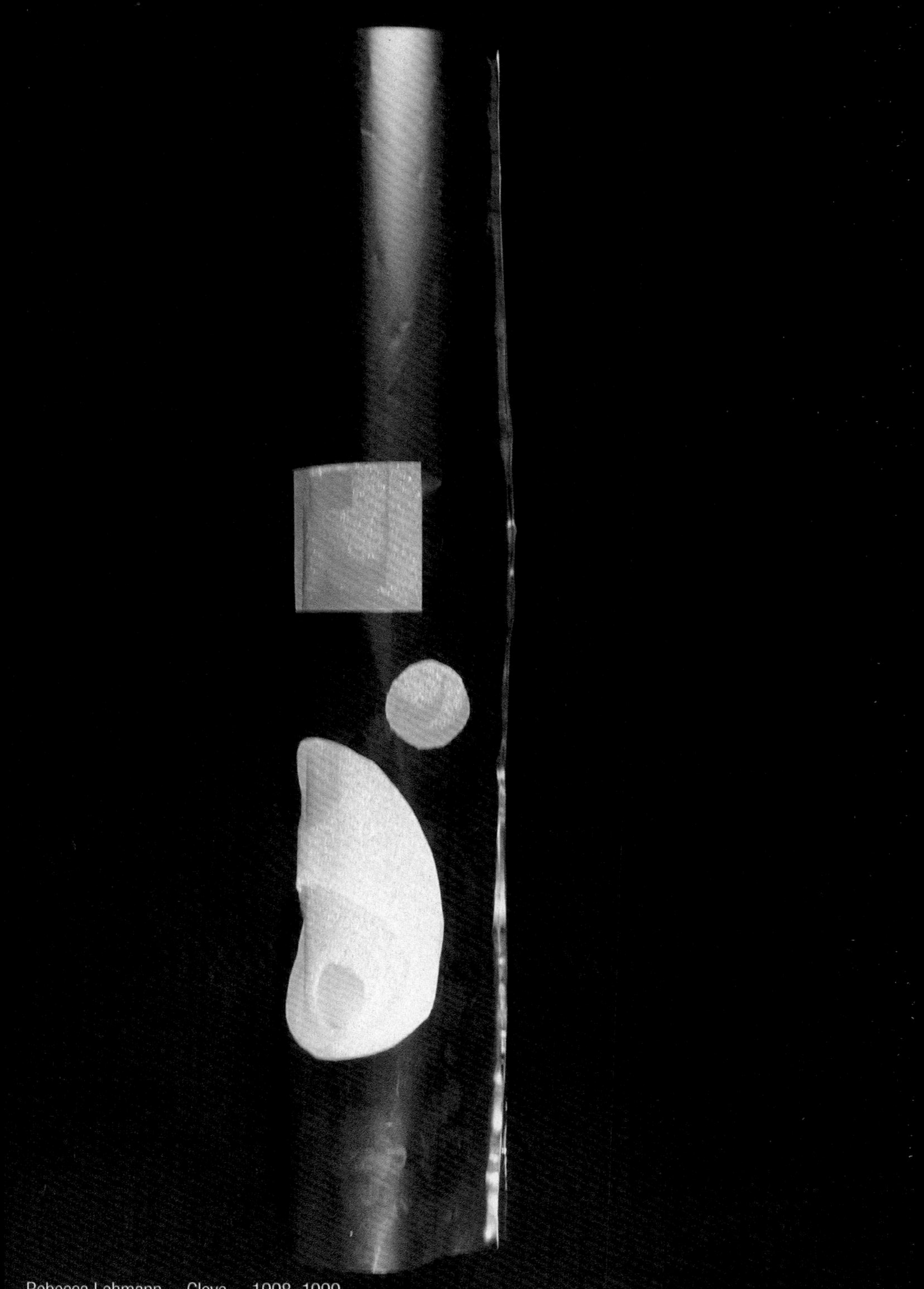

Rebecca Lehmann Glove 1998–1999

Sabrina Frank Räumling 1999–2000

Fabian Hilti, Marcel Marxer Structure 2001–2002

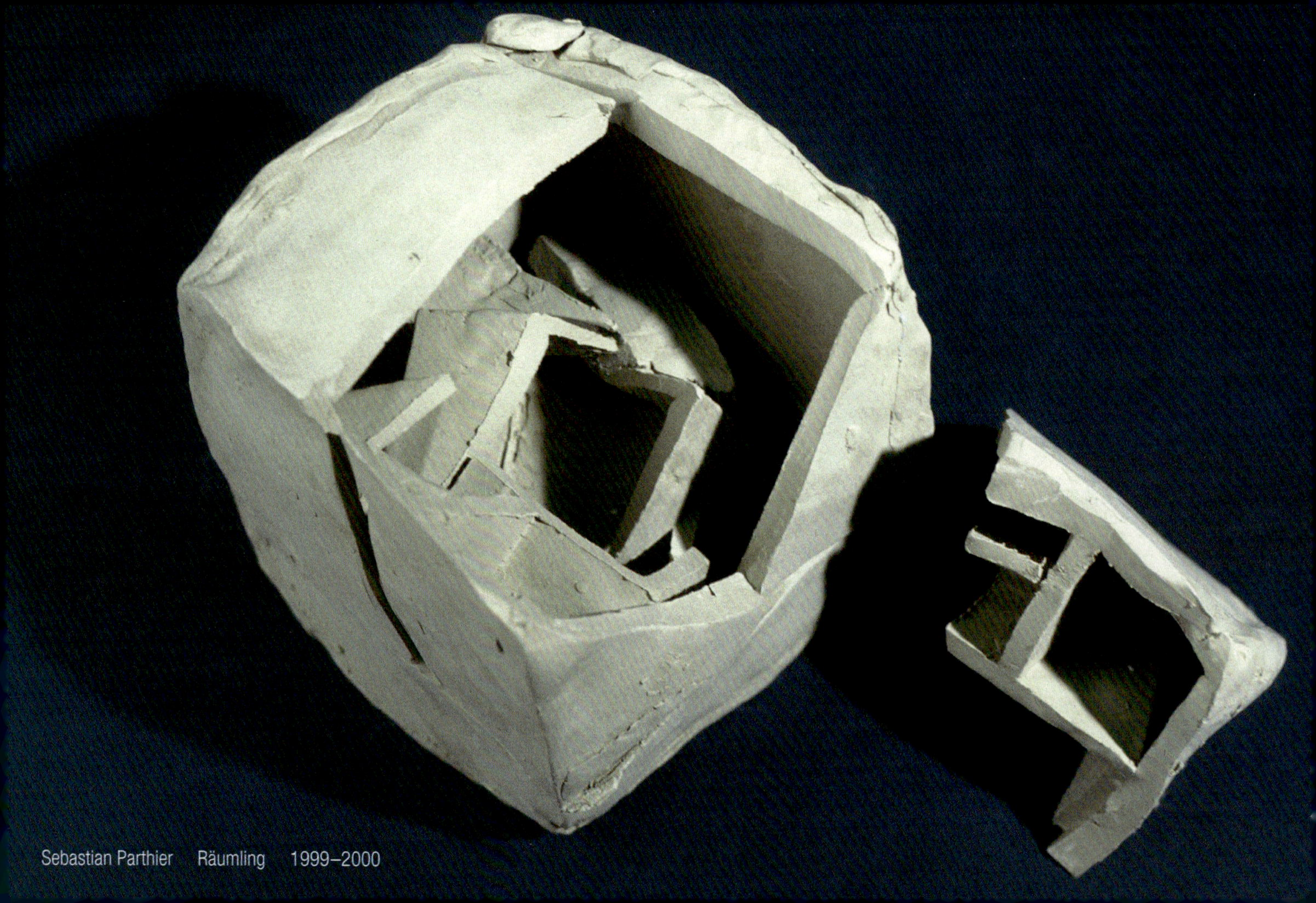

Sebastian Parthier Räumling 1999–2000

Sandra Hons, Claudia Loewe   Structure   1999–2000

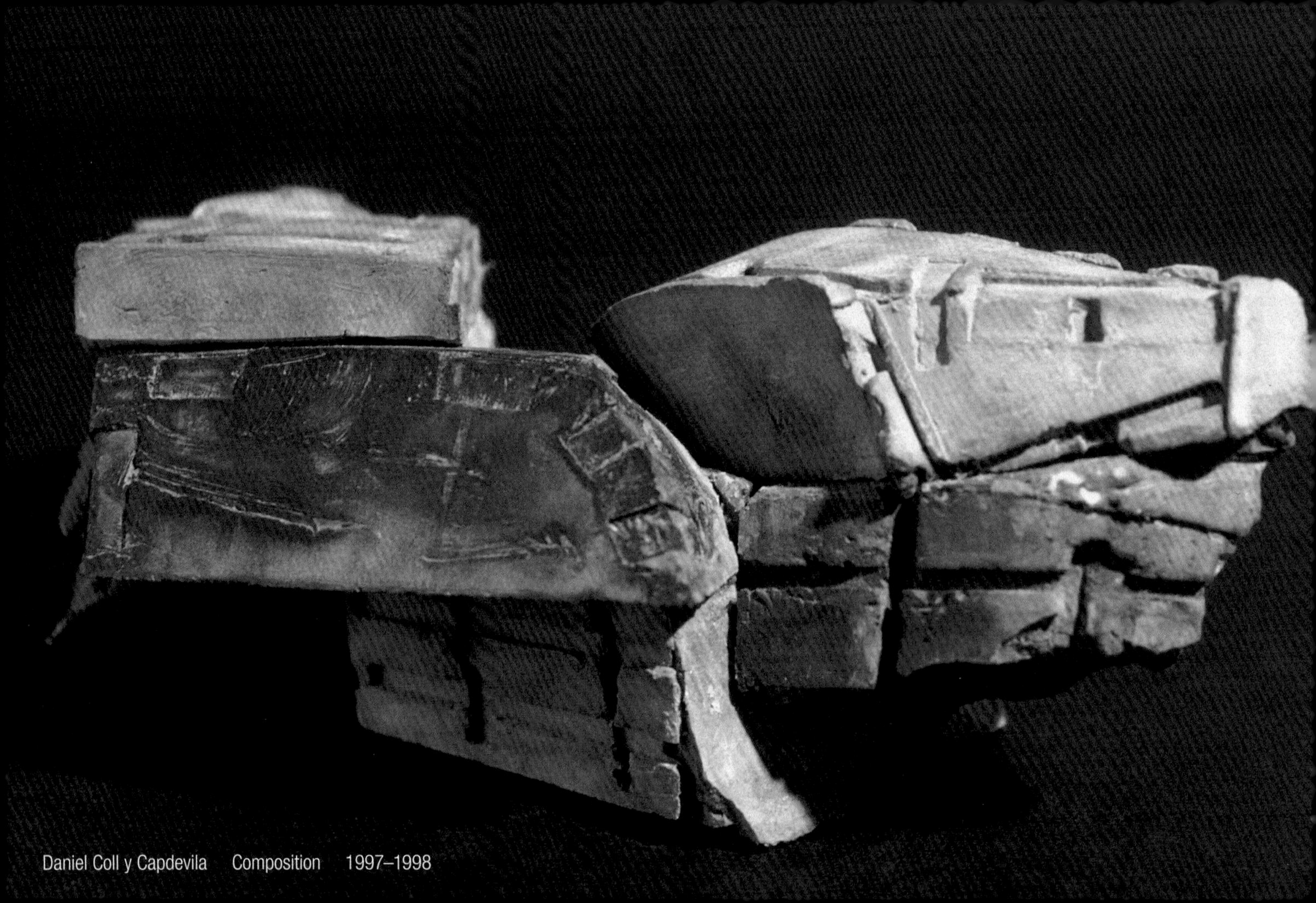

Daniel Coll y Capdevila Composition 1997–1998

Matej Draslar, Andreas Lochmatter   Building   2006–2007

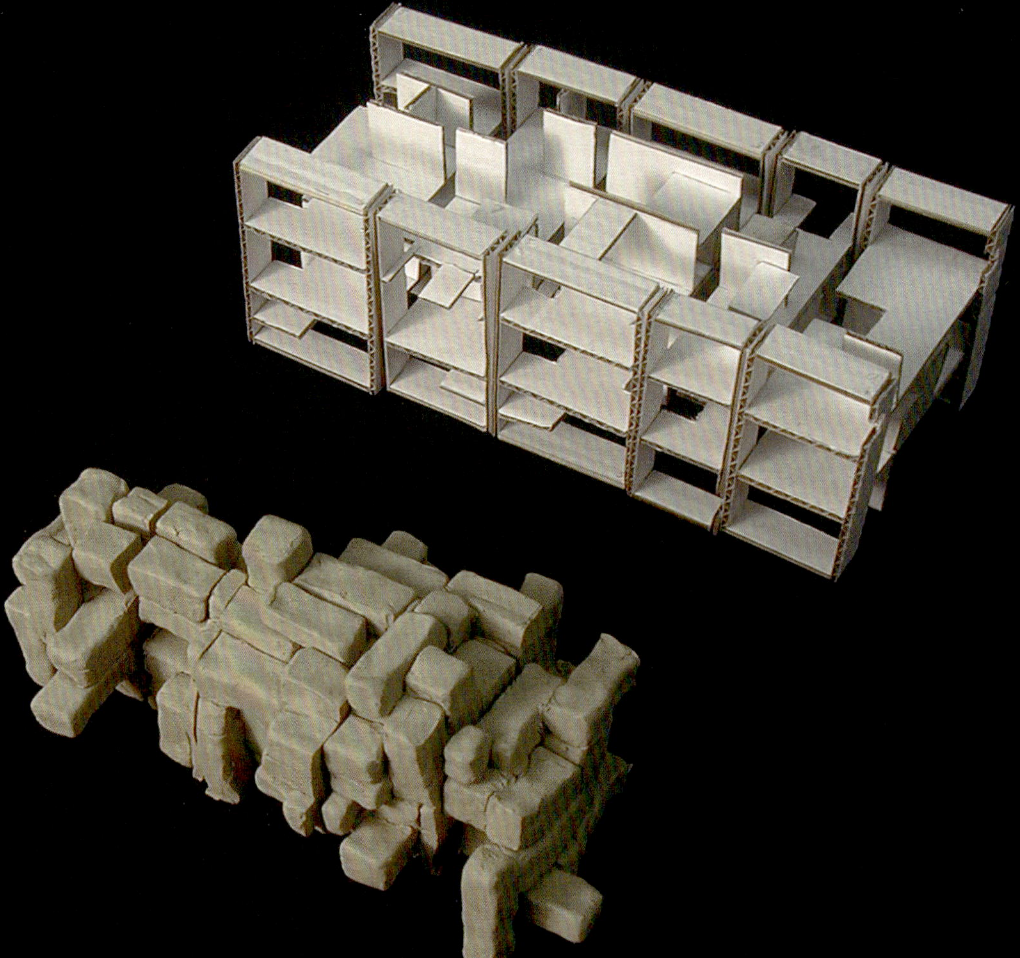

Evelyn Steiner, Yvonne Visintainer   Räumling / Transformation   2001–2002

Matej Draslar, Andreas Lochmatter Building 2006–2007

Katrin Gurtner, Peter Leibacher, Luca Pestalozzi, Jeanine Walther Prototype 2004–2005

Tian Chiang, Marie Eggenschwiller, Helen Munzinger, Nina Täschler   Eight-hour chair   2004–2005

Gabriel Calatrava, Marijke Ernst, Pascal Rosé, Matthias Stark, Carole Trachsel Prototype 2004–2005

Daniele Grambone, Benjamin Hohl, Cornelia Meier, Kerry de Zilva Eight-hour chair 2004–2005

Georg Krummenacher, Maike Schneider, Marina Stocker, Raphael Wicky Eight-hour chair 2004–2005

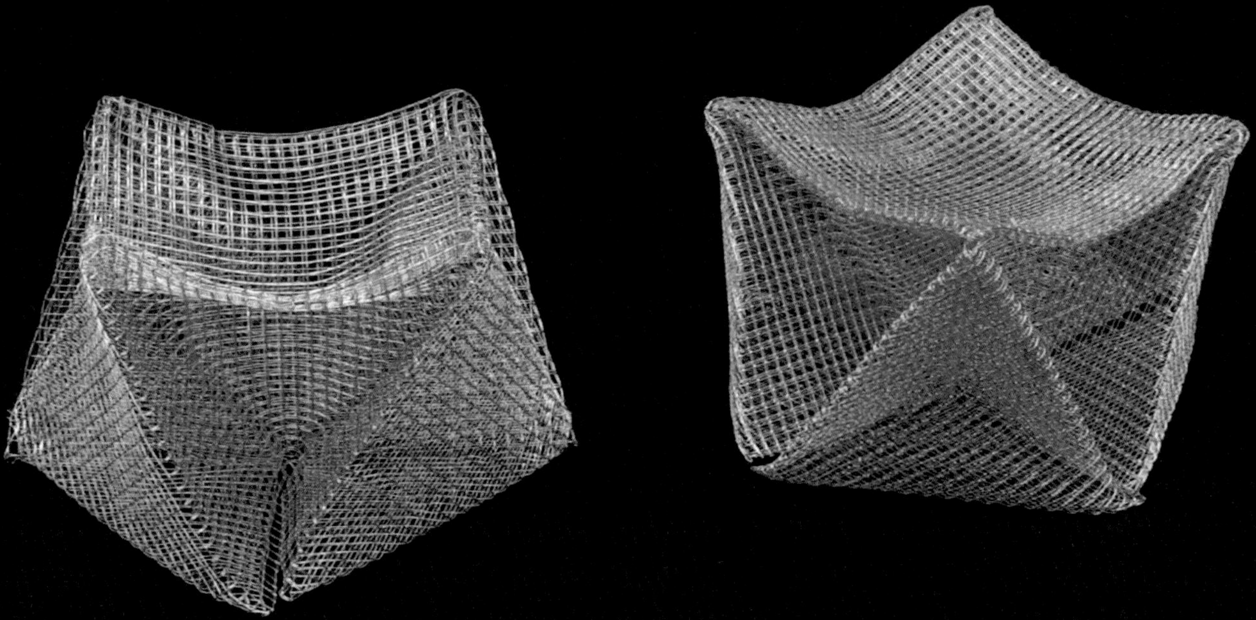

Andreas Aeschbacher, Olivier Blaser, Andrea Schregenberger, Esther Studer Eight-hour chair 2004–2005

Mirco Cortesi, Caroline Goeser, Faye Märki, Daria Rhyner Eight-hour chair 2006–2007

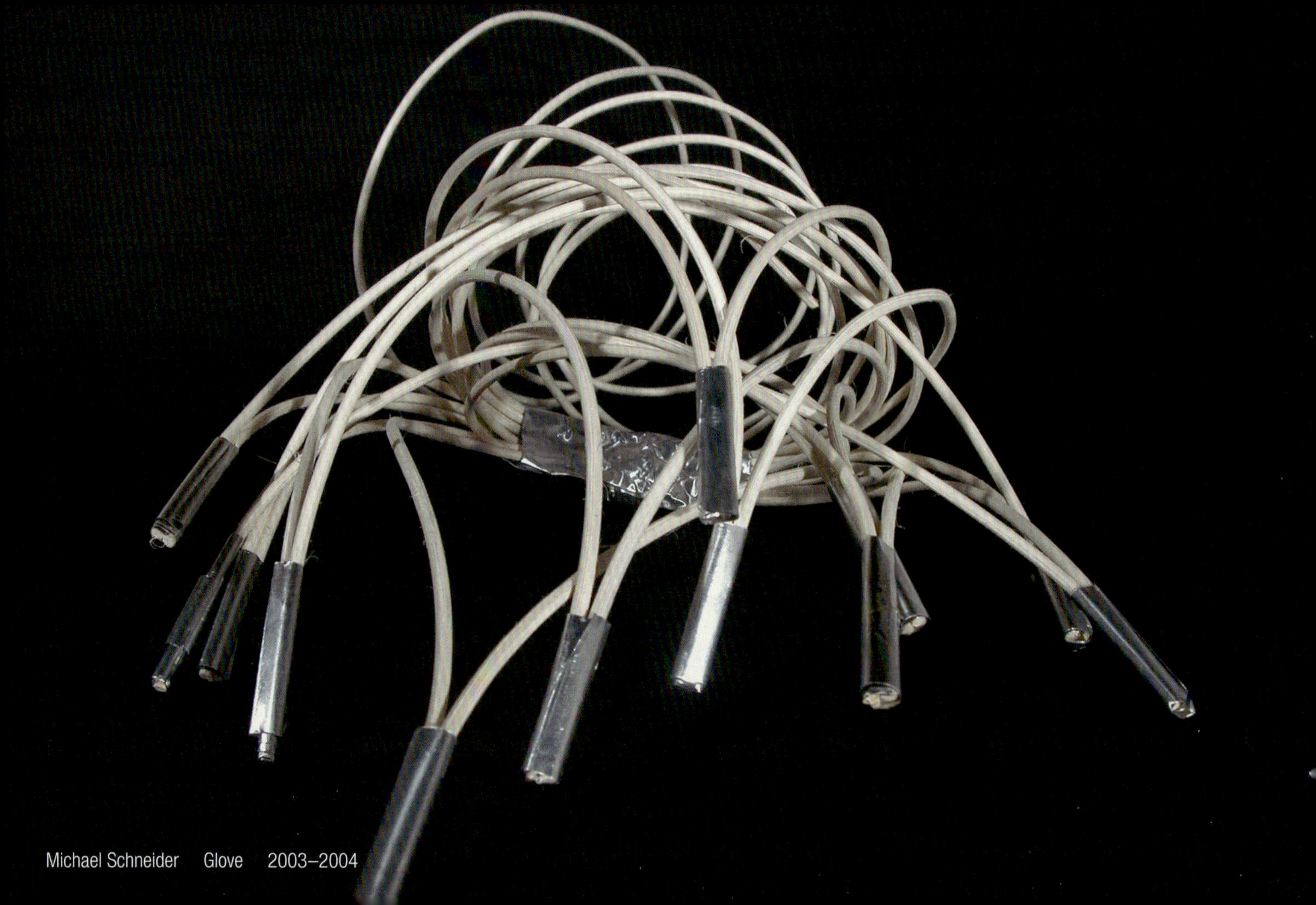

Michael Schneider Glove 2003–2004

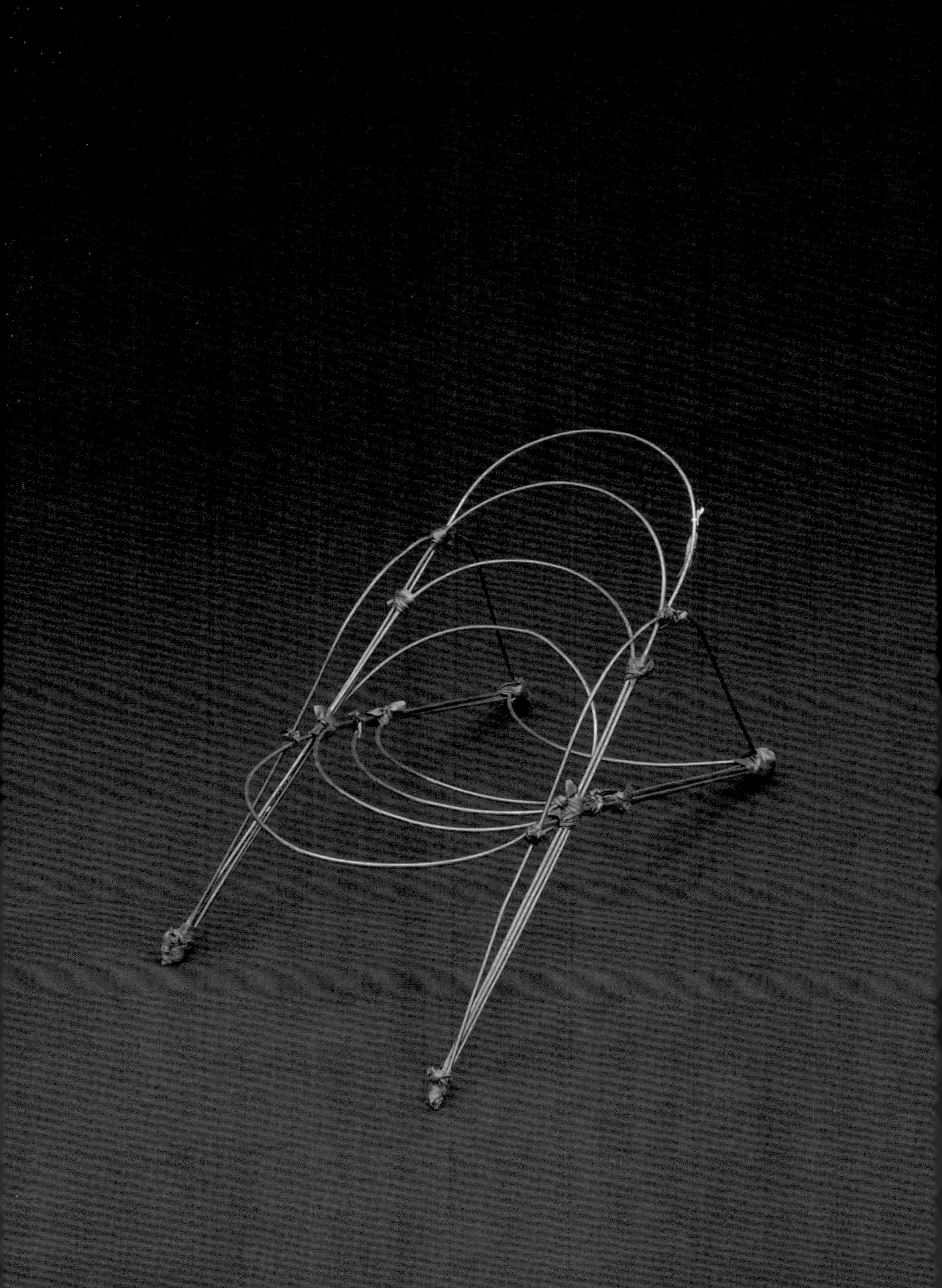

Angela Müller, David Ritz, Karin von Wyl   Prototype   2004–2005

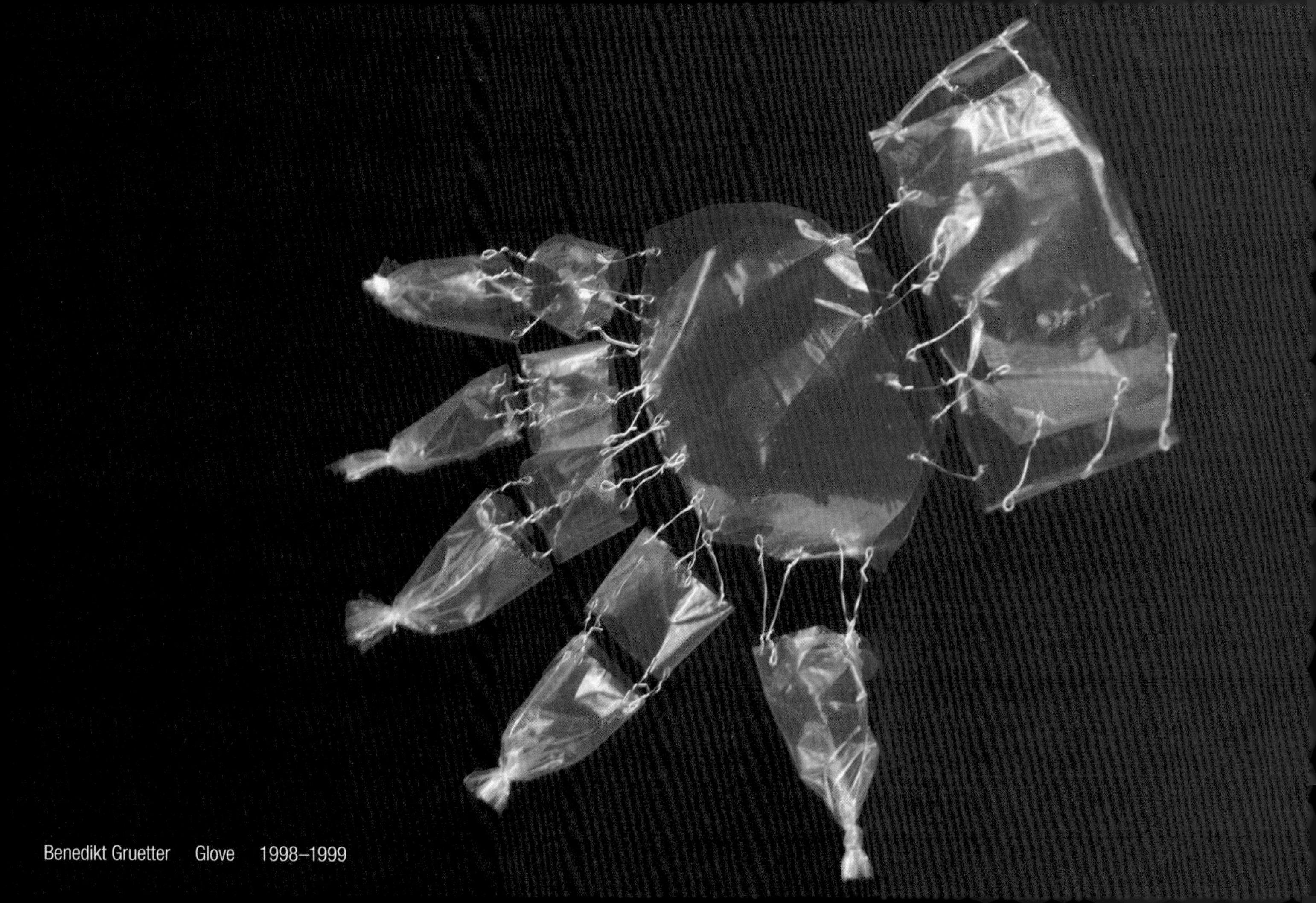

Benedikt Gruetter Glove 1998–1999

Tobias Friedli, Alexander Marty, Fabian Schärer, Philip Weber Eight-hour chair 2006–2007

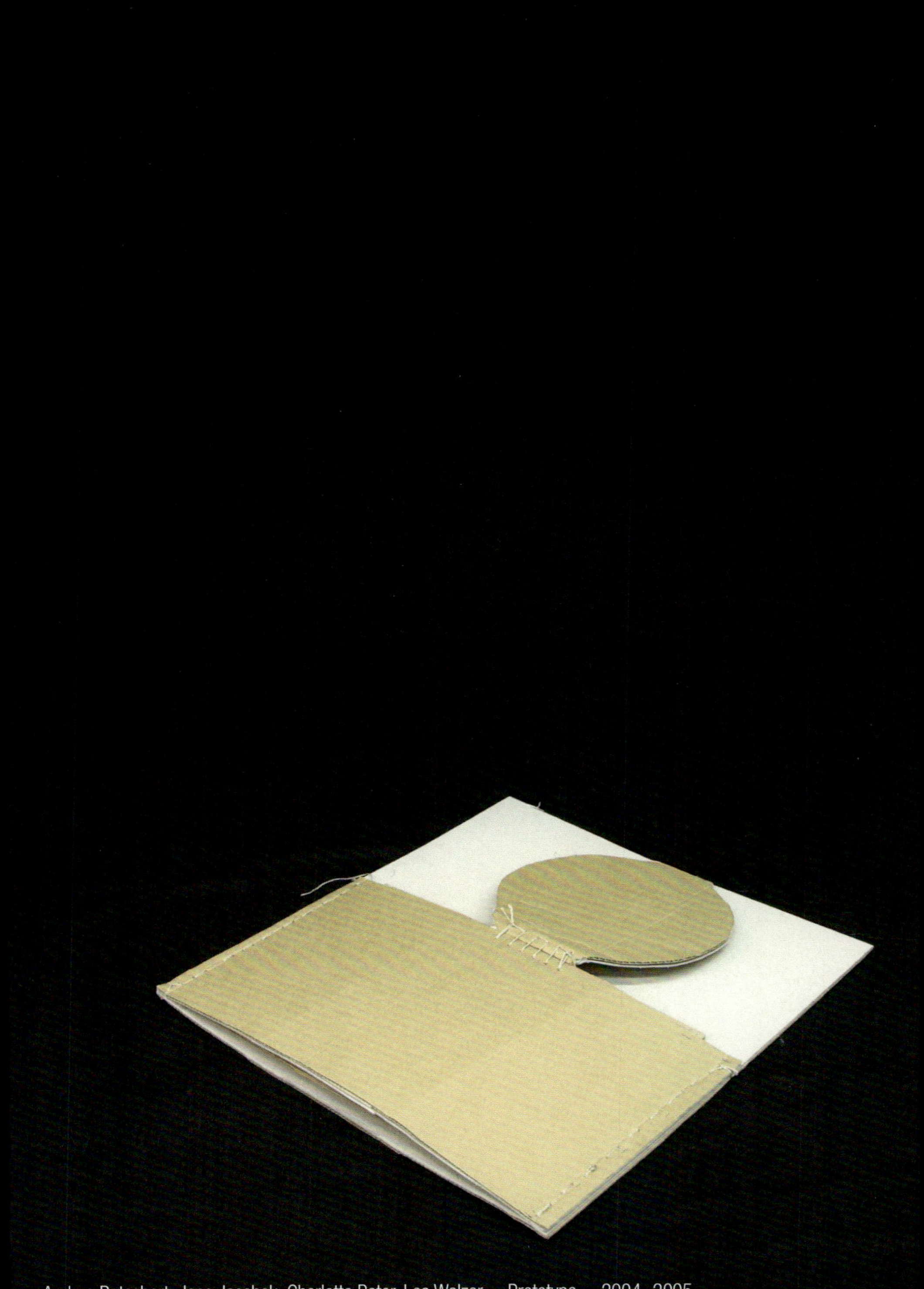

Andrea Betschart, Jens Jaschek, Charlotte Peter, Lea Walzer Prototype 2004–2005

Matthias P. Alder, Jennifer Karrer, Eva Lanter, Pascal Steiner

Eight-hour chair

2006–2007

Andreas Egolf, Jonas Kaufmann, Fabian Landolt, Nicolas Mentha Prototype 2004–2005

Samuel Smith, Lea Stocker Constructive project 2005–2006

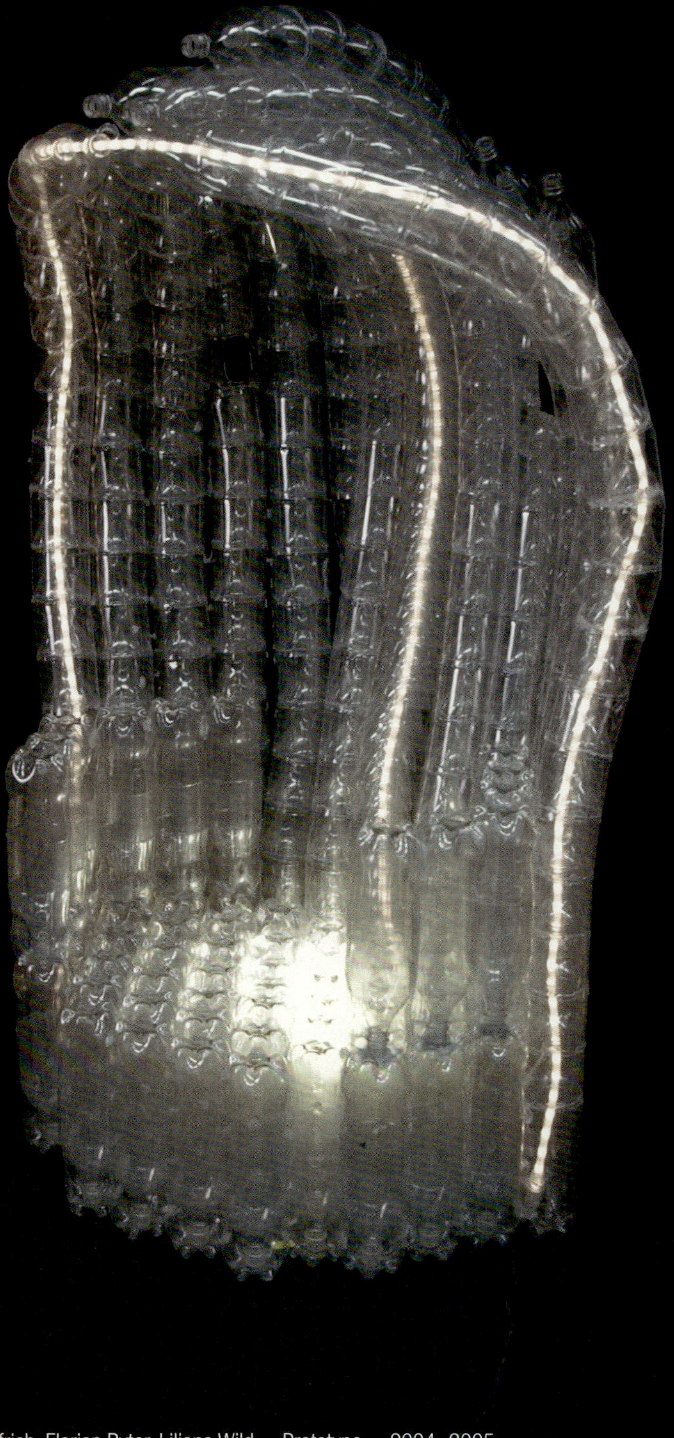

Raphael Broz, Kaspar Helfrich, Florian Ryter, Liliana Wild   Prototype   2004–2005

Dominik Aegerter, Naomi Hanakata, Franziska Singer Eight-hour chair 2004–2005

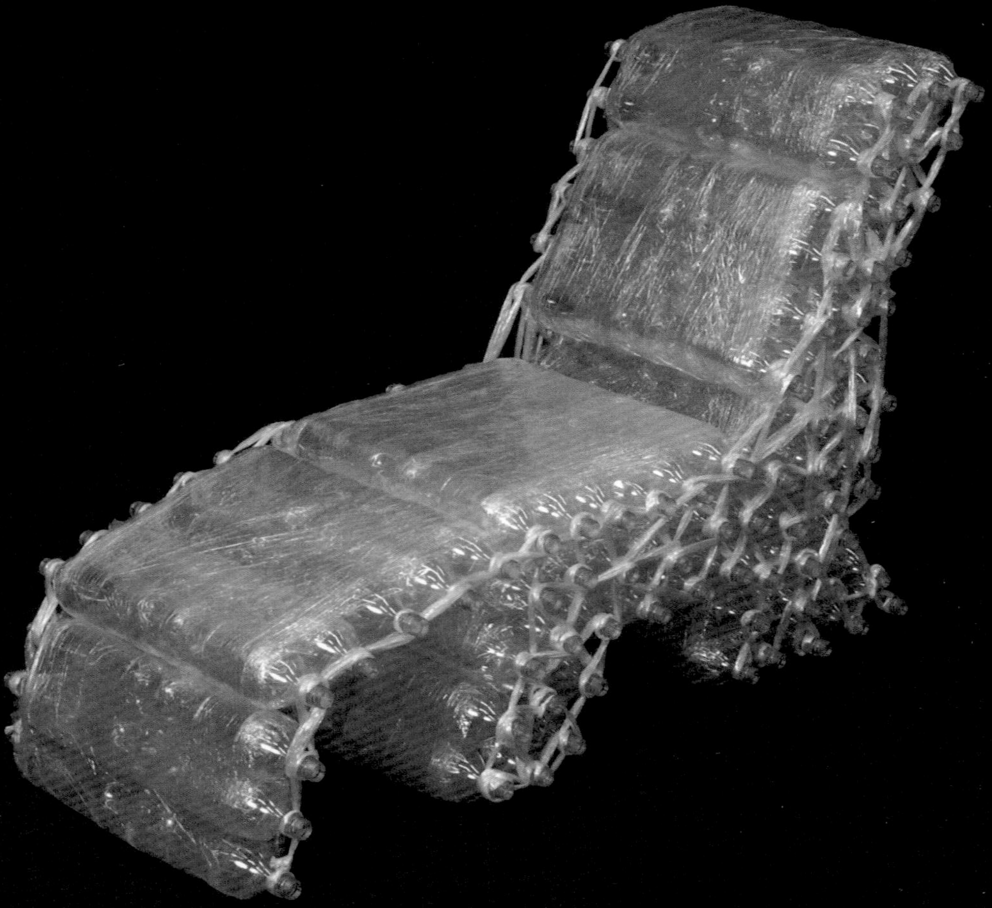

David Föhn, Philip Haspra, Thomas Hofer, Samuele Tirendi Eight-hour chair 2005–2006

Fabian Diem, Jana Henschen, Patricia Holend, Melanie Tichelli Eight-hour chair 2006–2007

Elisa Forster, Matthias Knuser, Dario Rizzo, Andrei Zouev   Eight-hour chair   2006–2007

Corinne Huwyler, Christina Imfeld, Marilen Muff, Lisa Oberli Eight-hour chair 2005–2006

Andrea Buchmeier, Kaspar Howald, Andrea Jeger, Géraldine Meyer   Eight-hour chair   2006–2007

Fund Composition 1997–1998

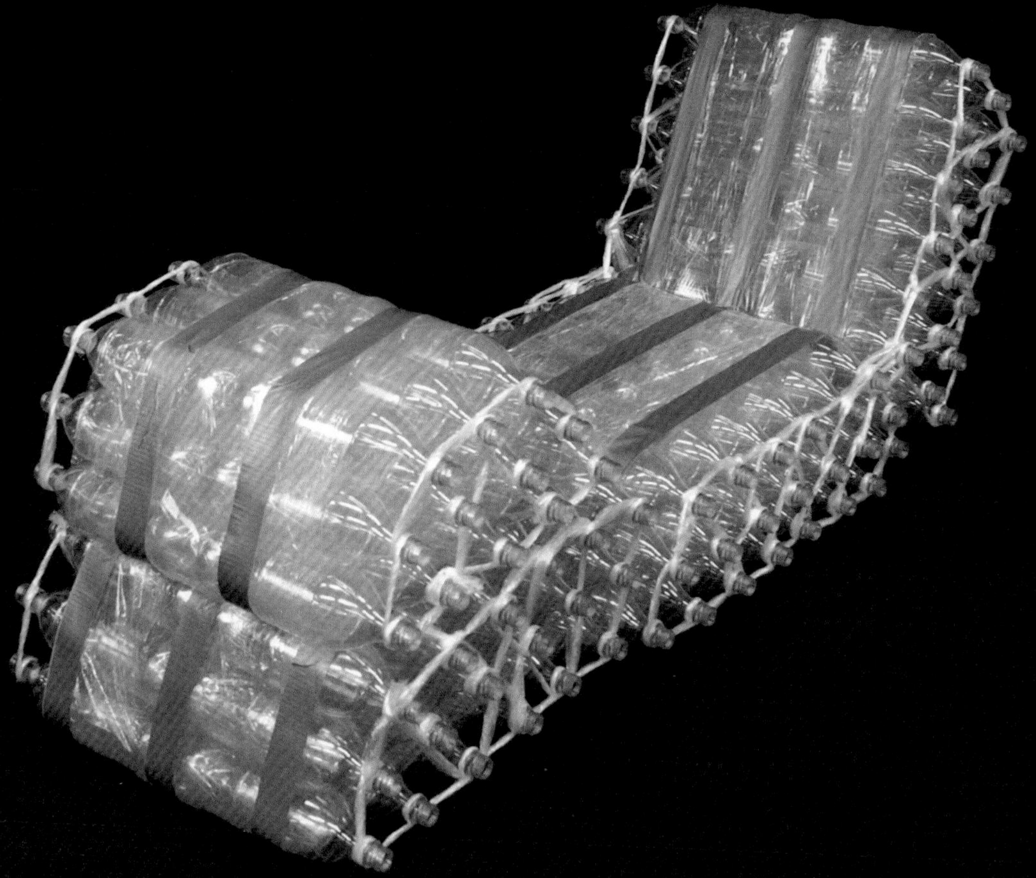

Dominik Aegerter, Naomi Hanakata, Franziska Singer   Prototype   2004–2005

Simone Blum, Christina Farragher, Lukas Prestele, Michael Trnka   Eight-hour chair   2006–2007

Simone Buchmann, Simon Kraus, Michael Reiterer, Zoran Spehar   Eight-hour chair   2005–2006

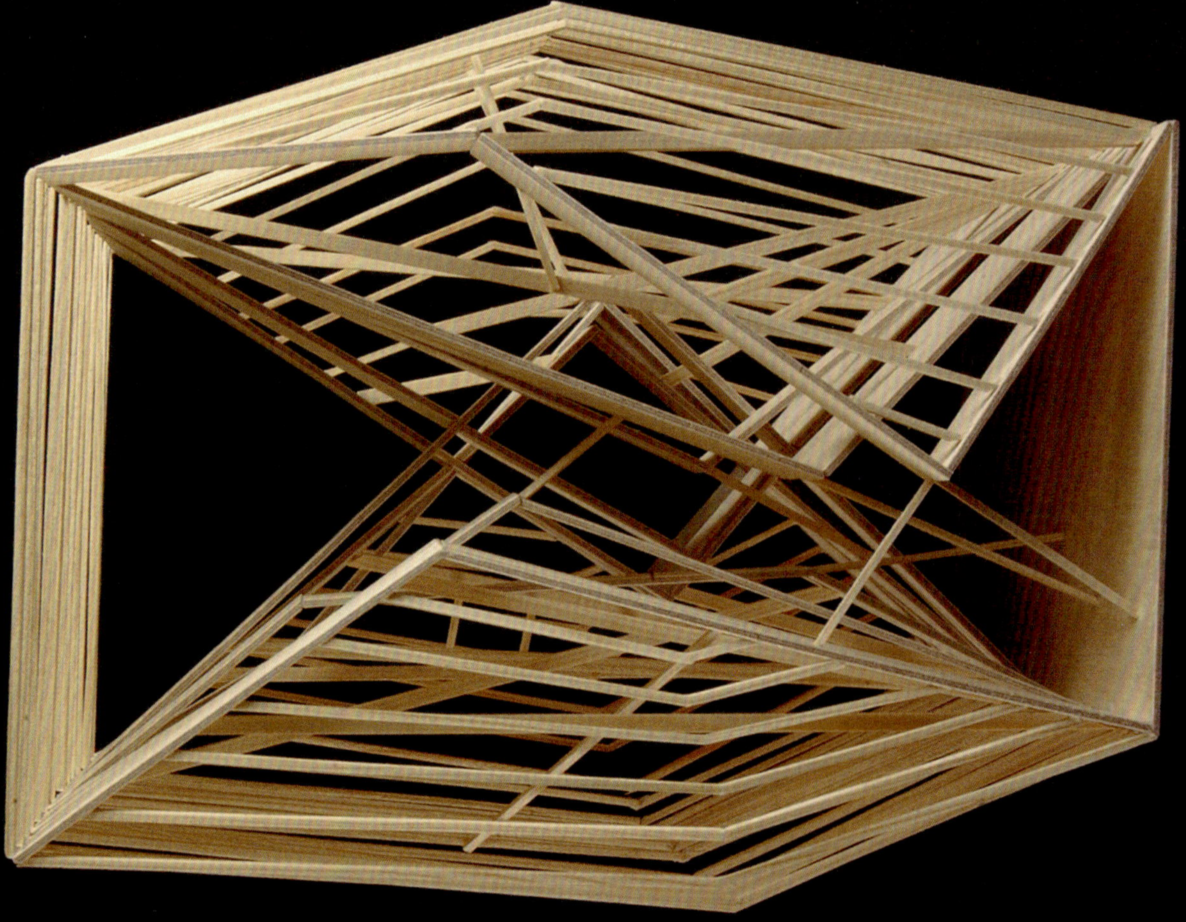

David Kühne, Noëmie Züst   Tectonics   2001–2002

Alexander Bürgi, Ursina Götz, Andreas Kaufmann, Sarah Schütz Eight-hour chair 2005–2006

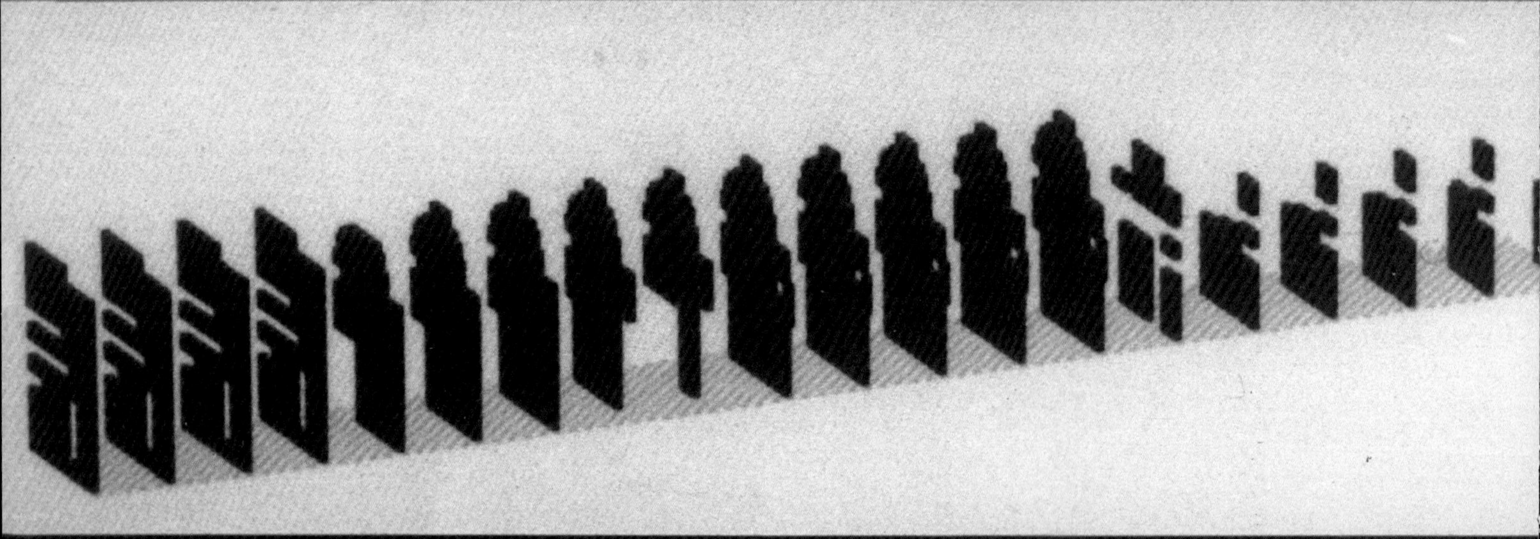

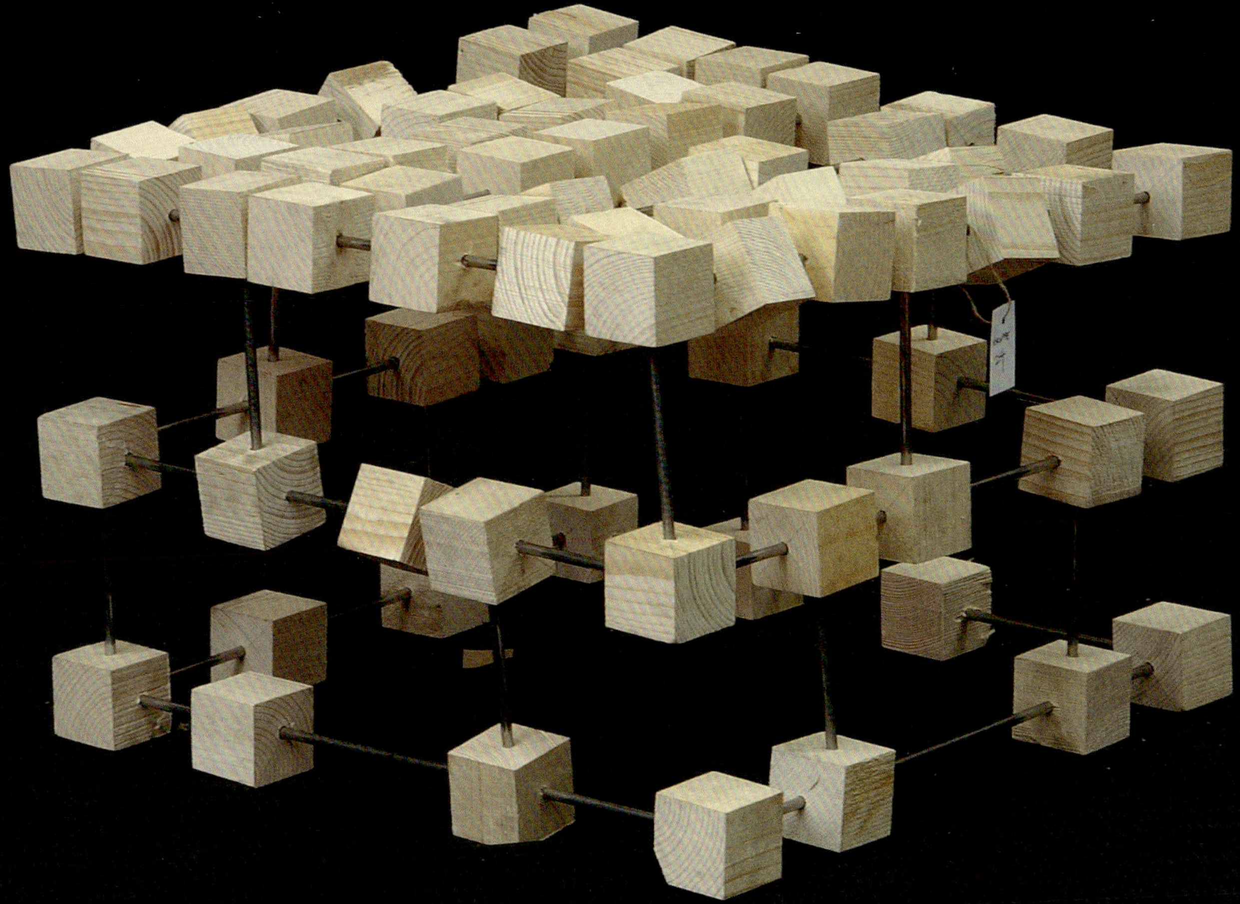

Rebecca Bornhauser, Rahel Gruber, Jessica Hevi, Silja Niederer   Eight-hour chair   2005–2006

Martina Friedli, Mischa Jäggi, Elina Müller, Adrian Rösli   Eight-hour chair   2006–2007

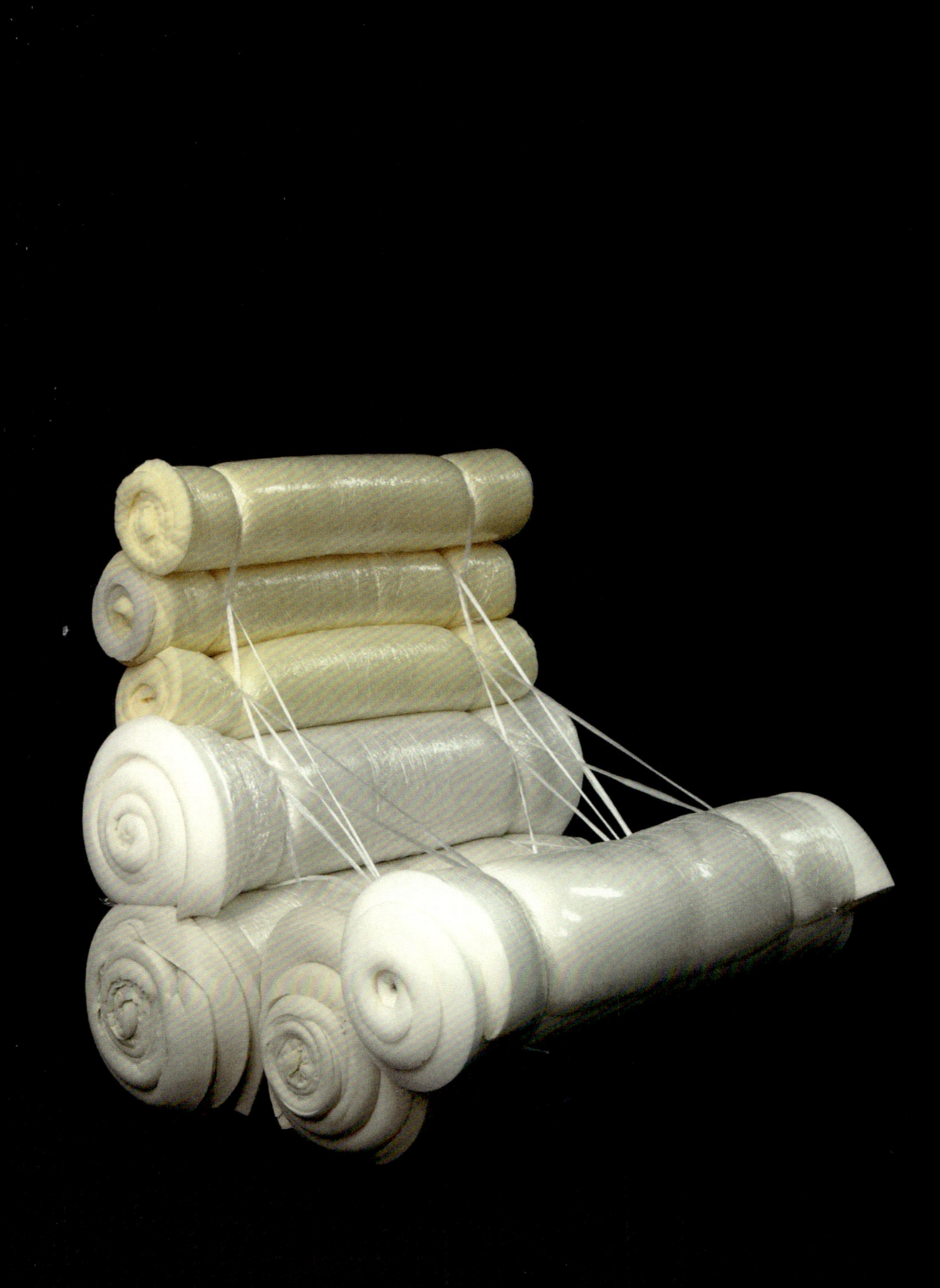

Marc Bill, Alexandra Blaser, Camilla Johansen Piltoft, Daniela Meyer Eight-hour chair 2005–2006

Sandro Agosti, Basil Spiess Constructive project 2002–2003

Jakob Heer, Caroline Zimmerli   Constructive project   2000–2001

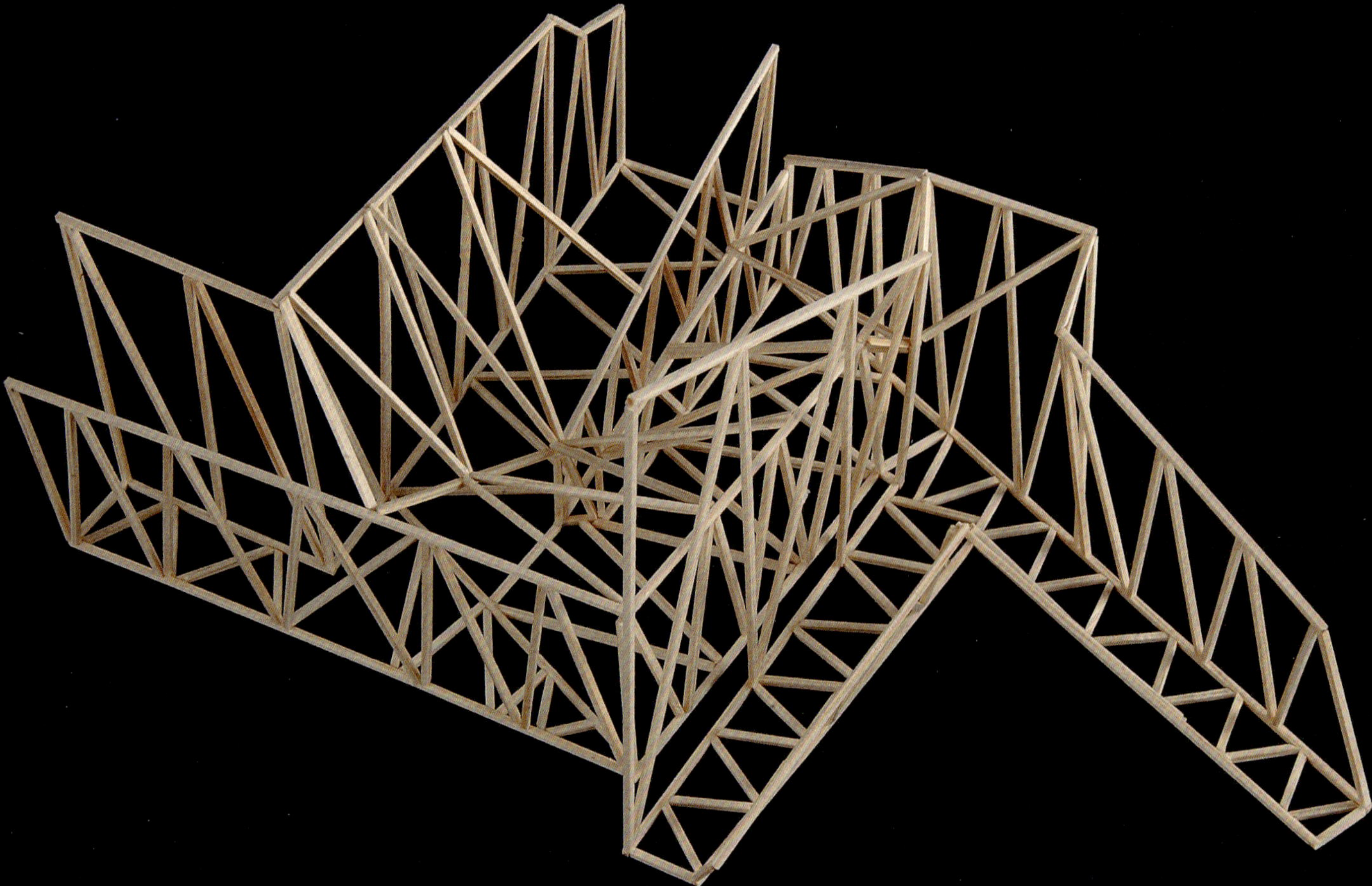

Niklaus Achermann, Corinne Lehner   Structure   2002–2003

Philipp Eigenmann, Andreas Ruch   Constructive project   2005–2006

Rebecca Bornhauser, Claudia Lehmann   Building   2005–2006

Lukas Burkhart, Nicolas Rothenbühler, Rahel Urech-Somogyi, Vladimir Vlajnic Eight-hour chair 2006–2007

Lukas Kissling, Hans-Peter Müller   Building   2006–2007

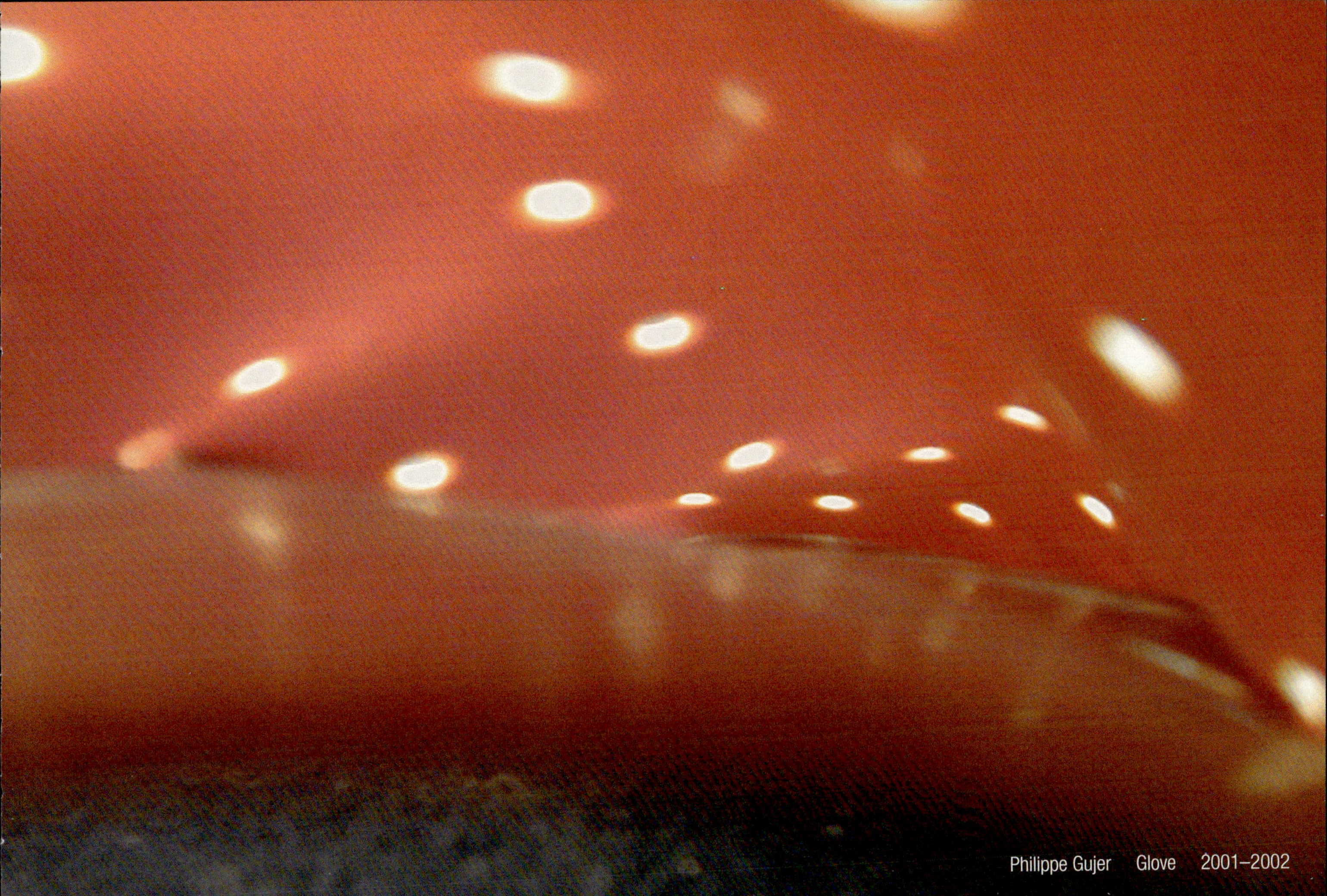

Philippe Gujer Glove 2001–2002

Platform Building 2006–2007

Submissions First-Year Course 1997–2007

Winter semester 1997–2003

- Glove
- Räumling (Space creature)
  Disassembling
- Transformation
- Tomography
- Mold.Pouring
- Composition
- Structure
- Tectonics
  Tectonics.Space
  Tectonics.Material

Winter semester 2004–2007

- Eight-hour chair
- Reflection
- Systematization
- Connection
- Structure
- Support
- Space
- Shell
- Building plan
- Building

Summer semester 1997–2007

- reConstruction
  reConstruction.Analysis
  reConstruktion.Synthesis
- Constructive project
  Constructive project.Research
  Constructive project.Concept
  Constructive project.Project

Winter semester 1997–2003

Glove

We have put together for you materials with diverse qualities: on the one hand, rigid materials, and on the other hand, non-rigid materials. From these choices, select two materials. Using only those materials you have chosen, design a glove without any additional means of fastening that can be taken on and off.

Think about the hand and its wealth of abilities. Are you interested in the active or passive hand? Beginning with the hand's diverse qualities, examine the principles of its covering and what it expresses. In your presentation, succinctly describe the spatial aspects, the ways the materials are joined and the relationship between wearing and covering.

Submission: glove; individual work, 1 day.

Räumling (Space creature)

You receive a certain amount of clay. Shape a contiguous sculptural form that allows an inner space to develop. Use all of the clay at your disposal. Work with your hands and the tools. Sound out the possibilities of the material and in doing so, allow for the creation of space. While working on the *Räumling*, turn it and observe it from all sides. Knead it, model it, and distort it. In brief: "think" by "doing". What strategies are at the base of your work? What spatial qualities emerge in your object? Sketch out your findings.

Disassembling

Consider how to dissect your *Räumling* into five parts without any residual pieces. Select the location of the slices so that the previously described spatial qualities become visible, and so that you can once again reassemble the *Räumling* back to its original form.

Before slicing the *Räumling*, hand draw a diagrammatic, alleged sectional view of two of the slices. In doing so, clearly differentiate between the parts that are space and those that are mass.

When the clay has sufficiently hardened, carry out your cuts cleanly and precisely. Afterwards, lay out the parts individually to dry.

Submission: *Räumling* of clay, fitting together the five dried parts with elastic bands, sectional view drawings, sketch book; individual work, 1 day.

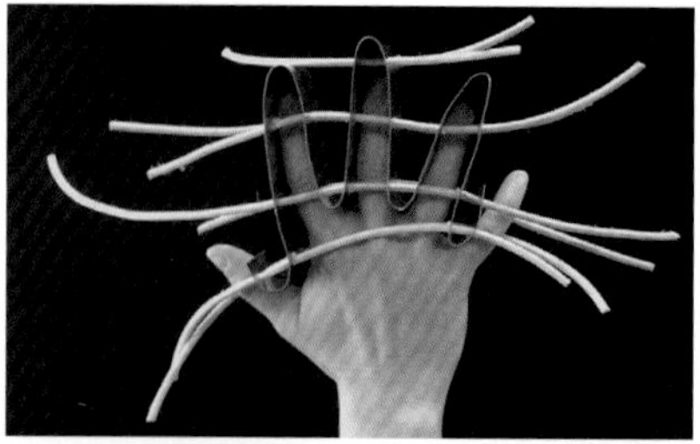

Glove. Saratz Marchet
2001–2002

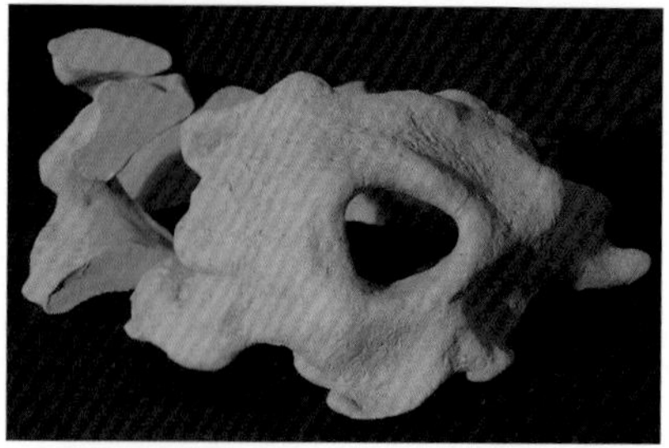

Räumling. Fabian Valverde, Thomas Wölfel
2001–2002

Disassembling / Transformation. Angela Sachs
2003–2004

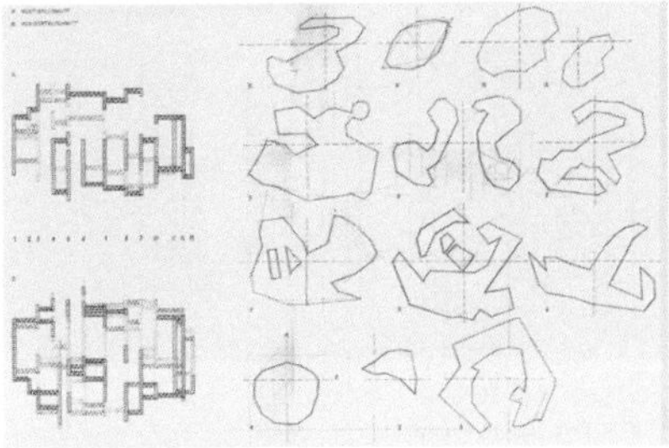

Tomography. Corinne Weber
2003–2004

Transformation

Build the five individual parts of the clay *Räumling* out of cardboard, true to scale. At this juncture, reconstruct the principles of your *Räumling* along the lines of a clarifying enhancement. Use the qualities of the cardboard appropriately, so that it supports your spatial, structural, and constructive intentions or first makes them possible. Think about the firmness and strength of the material, about the development of the front side and the edges. We will provide you with both chipboard and corrugated cardboard. You can use both types of board, especially for creating a clarifying hierarchy. Avoid any decorative use of the material.

Think in sketches about the various types of realizations in board material. Use key words to cite the criteria for your construction decisions.

Submission: assembly-ready model of cardboard in five parts, scans of "sliced" parts, sketch book; individual work, 1 day.

Tomography

Use a drawn plan to explain the essential conceptual contents of your reassembled cardboard *Räumling*. Focus here is the spatial, structural, and constructive qualities of your three-dimensional structure. Draw true to scale, but for better articulation of your concept, again carry out changes that lead to more clarity. Do not draw "symbolically" or pictographically, but exclusively (archi)tectonically, which means, correctly representing the materials in terms of their dimensions and the way they are joined together (like for an anatomical specimen).

Submission: drawings, pencil on drafting paper; individual work, 1 day.

Mold.Pouring

Prepare appropriate parts of your cardboard *Räumling* to serve as a mold and fill them. In the end, there should be five cast parts.

You have various possibilities for obtaining a completed cast form from the *Räumling's* parts. Enclose open bits of the form with a sheet of cardboard or put together separate parts of the *Räumling*. Also think about whether cardboard sheets should be removed or added. What you include in the mold will be impressed in the casting mold: sheets of cardboard will later become gaps; cardboard volumes will become cavities and tun-

nels (hollows). Various surfaces and depressions arise when you work on or overlay the cardboard. The mold forms must be airtight and painted entirely with glycerin before being poured.
For documentation, take photos of the cardboard *Räumling*, the molds, and the cast parts and sketch the actions with which the cast parts arose, or the rules used for making them.
Submission: 5 cast parts, photos, sketch book; individual work, 1 day.

Composition

Select five cast parts from the ten available and put together an architectural model by joining the parts and six sheets of chipboard to a new whole. For this, it is possible to clip or fold the boards, but not cut them up. Introduce the scale of 1:100 for the object and attempt to transfer yourself to the spaces that arise.
Develop a strategy for joining. The parts can be pushed against one another, wedged together, interlocked, layered, placed on top of one another, or arranged side by side. And you can include gaps, interstitial spaces, and cavities. Make sure that the composition is coherent as a whole, and that it holds together without any additional means of fastening – apart from glue.
Describe the relationship of hollow space to mass, the relationship of the parts to one another, as well as to the whole. Do hierarchies or spatial sequences emerge? Record the qualities by means of architectural drawings (building instructions, horizontal and vertical sections, axonometry, or exploded view) and an expressive sketch of the interior.
Submission: composition, drawings, sketch book; team of 2 students, 1 day.

Structure

Concretize your composition in the form of an architectural structural model of beams and slabs – a load-bearing system that establishes structural and spatial hierarchies. When building, pay attention to the spatial connections, stability (bracing), and connections of components.
Sound out the possibilities of the compositional model: How do you interpret the mutual influence of the spaces, of the solid bodies, interstitial and hollow spaces? Does the composition's additive character remain preserved or is it overlaid with a new structure? Do you read each of the parts of the composition as individual spaces or are they further

Mould.Pouring. Patric Eckstein
1997–1998

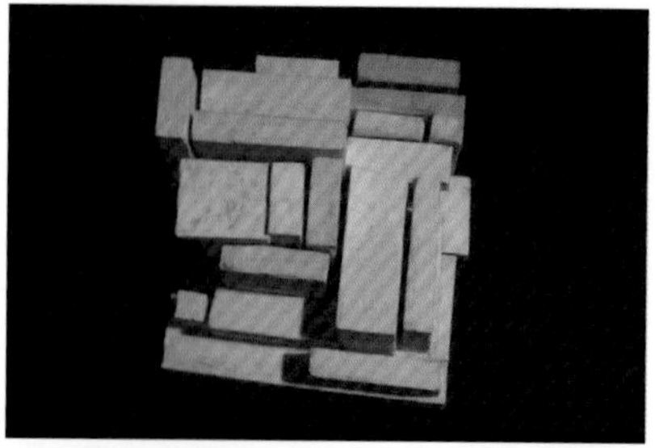

Composition. Regula Zwicky
1997–1998

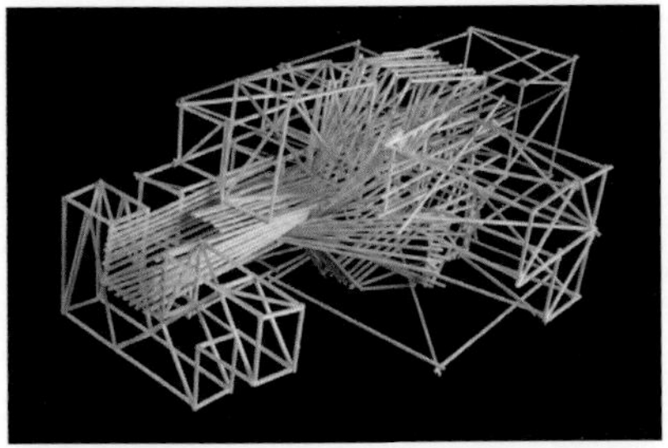

Structure. Dan Baciu, Ariel Burt
2002–2003

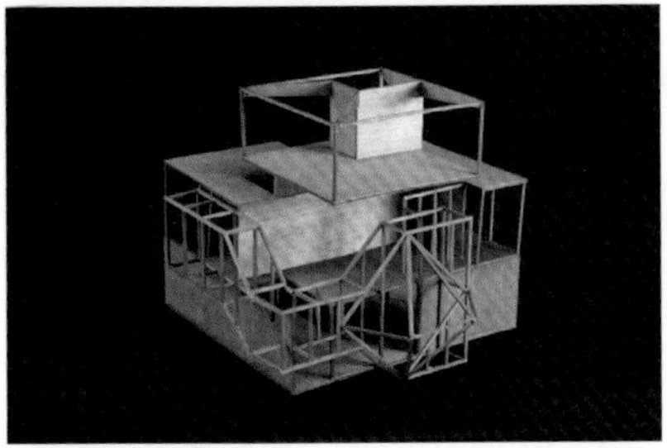

Tectonics. Adrian Fergg, Simon Fischer
2001–2002

subdivided into chambers or stories? Can their interfaces be clearly displayed, dissolved, or condensed? Determine the base of the structural model and with that, define the horizontal and vertical alignment.

Replicate the newly conceived structure at a scale of 2:1. Set priorities in dealing with primary and secondary structures as well as with the orientation of the slabs and beams (non-directional and directional structures). Likewise, hierarchies in the use of beams and slabs are to be examined, and corresponding relevant intersections explained and recorded.

Submission: structure model, work and concept drafts, sketch book, photos; team of 2 students, 3 days.

Tectonics.Space

In the following three-week exercise you develop a temporary shelter. It should provide a limited number of people a place to spend the night in sleeping bags, inexpensively, but nonetheless protected from the weather. We are concerned with the themes of space, and limiting and connecting it, site development, path, and light. A small piece of architecture arises in the synthesis.

Whereas with composition models, focus is directed towards questions of bodies, volumes, and surfaces, and with structure models, towards static issues and ability to join, you now examine your construct in terms of its three-dimensional qualities. To what extent are they already recognizable, how can they be intensified or created?

First, examine with the help of sketches drawn to scale, how the extremely simple program, which contains just a few designated uses, such as weather protection, accommodation, and retreat, finds expression spatially. How do the visitors enter the building? Where are the areas for lying down? How are they accessible? How do the guests move through the spaces?

In a further step, explain three-dimensional aspects of your project. How do the spaces connect with one another or how can they be bordered off from one another? Are the spaces strictly bordered, open, or flowing? Are the space-delineating areas closed or transparent? How are the spaces lit? Prepare a working model for this at a scale of 1:50 that provides information on the relationship of the spaces to one another and in opposition to the exterior.

Explain your project idea and develop it further. Decisions that have already been made should be questioned; sensible changes are entirely conceivable. For example, the project can be made smaller, i.e., "weak" parts can be removed. The stringent insertion of the access, in particular, will necessitate adjustments.

Tectonics.Material

The second step of the three-week exercise is concerned with the selection of material for your design. Examine your structural and spatial models to deduce a concrete, sensible material concept for the load-bearing and three-dimensional structure.
Is your project already so highly developed that a clear material concept can be implemented or do you need to make further specifications in the direction of a coherent overall concept? Formulate the criteria and conditions relevant in the choice of material: Do you recognize clear key areas in your models that demand certain material qualities? What materials are suitable in your specific case? Are there elements that can be realized only with certain building materials? What is basic structure? What is facing?
With the material concept, you now have, along with the structure, space, and program, four focuses for your design. In the last phase, develop your approaches to an architectural project. Pay attention to the hierarchical assembly of the components and the dimensioning of the materials.
Submission: tectonic model, interior photo, drawings, concept sketches; team of 2 students, 3 days.

Eight-hour chair. Jonathan Chaclan, Myra Kamber, Tania Tribelhorn, Gregor Vollenweider
2006–2007

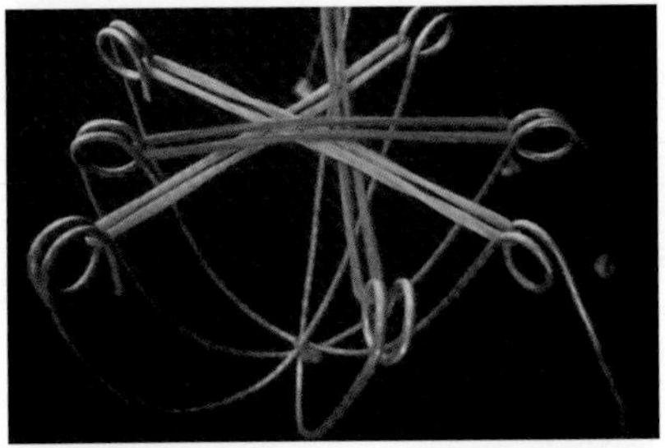

Reflection. Unknown author
2004–2005

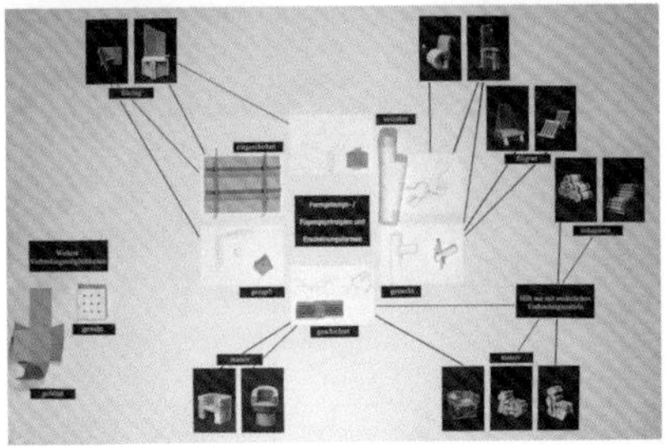

Systematization. Unknown author
2005–2006

Winter semester 2004–2007

Eight-hour chair

Construct a "fast" chair within eight hours. For this, we will provide you with materials with different qualities. You will be allocated one material at the beginning of the exercise, which you can supplement with an additional material of your choice. Construct the chair so that it is functional and able to bear your weight. Avoid any exclusively decorative or aesthetically motivated application of the materials. If possible, keep a photographic record of the working process.
Submission: chair; team of 4 students, 1 day.

Reflection

Examine and analyze the chair you constructed last week. Together with your team, describe and discuss its materialization, structure, and construction, as well as their mutual dependencies. Identify the structural and constructive principles, jointing and kinds of connections. Produce analytical sketches and diagrams of how the chair functions. From them, derive four simple concept models that either refer to different principles found in the eight-hour chair or describe variations of these principles.
Submission: concept models, sketches, and diagrams; team of 2 students, 1 day.

Systematization

Systemize the findings from the chair and reflection exercises by creating an overview in the form of a "field image". The base of the observations is formed by all of the chairs from the eight-hour chair exercise. Every group draws a lot with two themes that give their analysis a thematic framework. On the example of the themes, formulate more precise criteria that you will subsequently use for classification purposes. Subsequently choose 15–20 chairs that you consider exemplary and create a relationship among them. A personal "field image" emerges, a kind of relationship network with groups, sub-groups, cross references, multiple placements, etc. Conceive of the assignment playfully and discuss the arrangement.
Submission: field image; team of 2 students, 1 day.

Connection

Develop a construct based on the eight-hour chair or your findings from the reflection exercise. This construct should be created with the use of joining techniques such as sticking, braiding, knotting, layering, etc. The construct, which can be either rigid or flexible, provides information about the chosen connection technique. Experiment with material-specific qualities and make deliberate use of rigid or non-rigid materials. It is not necessary to use non-rigid materials exclusively for connection purposes, or rigid materials exclusively for framework. A maximum of two different materials are allowed for each model, whereby one of the two will be allotted by draw. The other material can be freely chosen from among the materials listed under jointing and fastening materials.
Submission: construct, sketches; individual work, 1 day.

Connection. Jennifer Karrer, Eva Lanter
2006–2007

Structure

Develop a three-dimensional structure model from one of your constructs from the previous exercise. Multiply your chosen principle inherent in the construct and subsequently join the elements together in order to get a structural arrangement. It is possible that simplification or reduction of the elements is necessary for the production of the "building blocks" in the new material.
During the building of the non-directional structure model, post binding rules that organize and stabilize it. Criteria for organizational principles are concepts such as chaotic–ordered, loose–dense, primary–secondary, centered–peripheral, two–three-dimensional, open–closed, etc. While working, discover the variety of organizational options and photograph the different possibilities.
Stability can be generated with the material itself, by folding, ribbing, or corrugating. Additional material enables the creation of stiffness through filling or spreading. In addition, the stiffness of the connection type plays an important role with regard to stability. The structure model should be stable, yet not exclude flexible joints.
Submission: structure model, sketches, model photos; team of 2 students, 1 day.

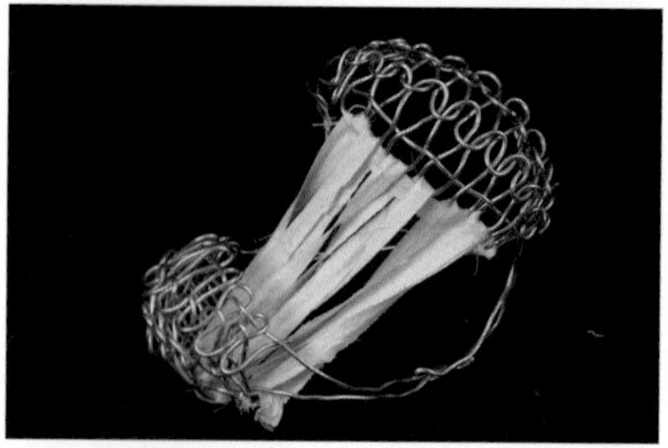

Structure. Gian Trachsler
2006–2007

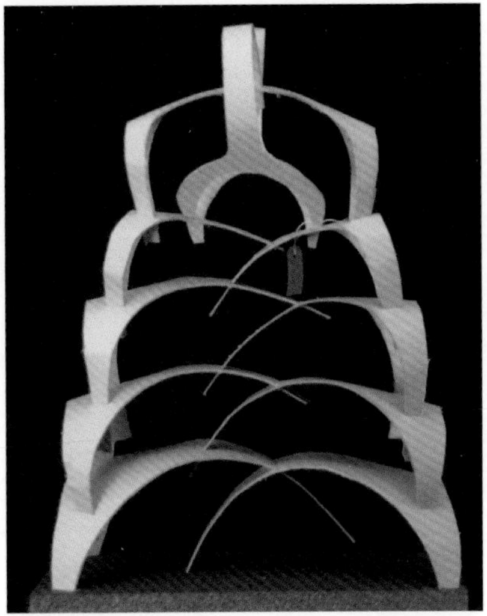

Support. Amélie Fibicher, Florence Herrmann
2005–2006

Space (molding). Manuela Ernst, Marion Heinzmann
2006–2007

Support

Develop a three-dimensional load-bearing structure model from the structure model of the previous exercise. Reduce or extend your structure, for example into a frame, shell, or slab construction, without forfeiting the model's individuality by doing so.
Your model now has a top and a bottom, i.e. it has a horizontal and a vertical load path. Consider how the loads will be transmitted, and establish which contributions are made by the individual parts for the load transmission or stiffening. Is it necessary to add stiffening measures to improve the vertical load transmission? Do you need stiffening, such as cardboard sheets or wire struts, in order to ensure the horizontal load-bearing ability? A further component of the assignment is presented by the optimization of the stability. Within the logics of the other elements, brace your load-bearing structure in such a way with the base plate made available to you to optimally direct the forces underground.
Submission: load-bearing model; team of 2 students, 1 day.

Space

In this step, a compact structure with a high degree of interior space should be developed. This space is subdivided in such a way as to produce a system of several connected but clearly demarcated or completely separated spaces. Each group experiments with one of three model construction techniques, which are representative of different solid construction techniques. Lots will be drawn for materials that stand for the forming, casting, and layering processes in solid construction. These processes correspond with techniques of plastic forming (Greek, plassein: to form, mold, design), or sculpture (Latin, sculpere: to cut, chisel, separate), which, to put it simply, corresponds with the addition or subtraction of formable material. Play with your allotted material and its inherent techniques and allow for spatial experiments. Finally, by cutting through it, expose the varied inner life of the spatial structure made of clay, plaster, or polystyrene.
Molding: You receive a specific amount of clay. Mold a coherent, plastic structure with complex interior space. Work with your hands, a spatula, or wire, and use all the clay at your disposal. Embark on a journey of discovery: add, mold, and discard. Finally, cut through the assembled object in a way that reveals the complex inner life of the object.
Layering: You receive a polystyrene slab measuring 1 x 60 x 125 centimeters. Cut the slab into pieces of 24 square centimeters. Use all the slab pieces and arrange them in lay-

ers. Arrange and join the individual pieces to form as compact as possible a whole with complex inner spaces. Consider what methods are inherent in this technique. Relief-like projections or set-backs, gaps, arches, or barrel and domical vaulting are some of the possibilities. Cut through the finished structure. You will then have two spatial shells. In the end, you fill their exposed inner spaces.
Casting: You receive a polystyrene block measuring 10x10x50 centimeters. Cut the block into five pieces, each with different dimensions, yet none smaller than 5x5x5 centimeters. Divide the block in such a way that no residual pieces remain. Order and join the individual pieces into as compact as possible a form by wedging them together, layering, or simply placing them on top of each other. Conceive the volume in all directions; there is no top or bottom, front or back. The outer dimensions should not exceed 20x20x25 centimeters. Produce a plaster volume by placing your polystyrene volume in a 20x20x25 centimeters cardboard box and subsequently pouring it with plaster. Since you want to acquire two cast sections, you must decide on an incision and place the cardboard sections in the negative form in such a way that when pouring you end up with two spatial shells.
Submission: three-dimensional object, shaped, layered, or poured; team of 2 students, 1 day.

Shell

The space exposed by means of a cut in the previous exercise is the basis of this exercise's spatial shell. Decide on the most interesting of the two shells and rebuild with the planar material the one half using corrugated cardboard. This step allows for various corrections: modify the given requirements in such a way that no dimension of the new shell exceeds 35 centimeters, but such that at least one of the dimensions complies with this length. In doing so, the proportions and specific qualities of the given model should be maintained.
Your model should be directional and should be read as a "mass with interior space". Decide accordingly for a top and a bottom. The new spatial shell must have at least two openings and three niches of different sizes and depths.
Submission: spatial shell model; teams of two students, 1 day.

Space (layering). Dominic Fierz, Mehran Rafati
2005–2006

Space (casting). Tobias Abegg, Christian Stark
2005–2006

Shell. Tobias Abegg, Christian Stark
2005–2006

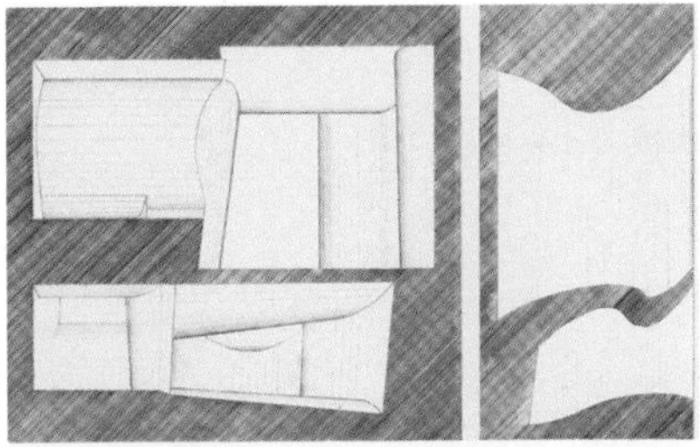

Building plan. Manuel Gander
2005–2006

Building. Emanuel Biland, Emmanuel Diserens
2005–2006

Building plan

Record the spatial shell of the previous exercise in a plan drawing: Create a horizontal and vertical section of the model. The vertical section corresponds with the section of the shell that you have already constructed, from which you can infer the exact dimensions. Make architectural drawings, i.e., portray the dimensions and manner of the cardboard construction accurately. From now on, consider the spatial shell as a definitive 1:50 model of a walk-in space. Where necessary, adapt room heights and niches to the dimensions of a human being.
Submission: section drawings on a scale of 1:50; individual work, 1 day.

Building

In the following three-week exercise you are asked to develop a free-standing building consisting of three to four rooms. The structure should have several stories encompassing vertical connections, such as ramps, stairways, and others.
In the following exercise, we are concerned with the themes of structure, construction type, space, access, and light. Context, topography, and specific uses play somewhat subordinate roles. Through the synthesis of the relevant themes a small work of architecture shall emerge.
The two models "space" and "shell" serve as sources of inspiration for the building, without it referring to them in terms of form. Consider what the essential characteristics of the two exercises are and how you can interpret them afresh. Such characteristics could be, for example, spatial principles (sequence, hierarchy, circulation), structural qualities (encapsulation, staggering, layering, kinds of openings), or atmospheric features (light, surface textures).
First of all, with the help of sketches and models made to scale, examine how the very simple program, which contains only a few requirements, influences your spatial concept. In the following week, further develop the spatial and structural aspects of your project with the same working methods. How does the structural implementation influence the spatial concept, and vice versa?
For the final submission, work out a materialization in accordance with your spatial concept and give it visible form with a tectonic model that uses minimal joining principles. You have the entire spectrum from solid to filigree construction at your disposal. The final

presentation is on a scale of 1:50 by means of powerfully expressive pencil drawings and the tectonic model.
Submission: tectonic model on a scale of 1:50, concept sketches, working models; team of 2 students, 3 weeks.

Summer semester 1997–2007

reConstruction.Analysis

The summer semester begins with the five-week exercise "reConstruction". In two blocks of exercises – a one-week analysis phase and a four-week synthesis and elaboration phase – six selected buildings will be examined and reconstructed. At the end of the exercise cycle, the work will be presented in plenum and commented on and discussed by invited experts.
Begin with the analysis of your building. For this purpose, work out statements on the following main themes:
– How is the building placed in the topography, how is it orientated, and how does it react in a constructional and scenic context?
– Describe space allocation and its spatial conception, and explore horizontal and vertical relationships between the spaces.
– What is the load-bearing structure like? Does it correspond with a building type? Which building materials were used? What is the relationship to space?
– How are the openings placed, and what are their characteristics? What relationship arises between interior and the exterior spaces? What is the character of the interior spaces, and how are the materials implemented? Are there any special lighting effects?
Make statements on these themes in the form of diagrams, precise sketches, perspectives, plans, photos, and references, or with models.
Submission: analyze presentation, models, sketches, and diagrams; team of 8 students, 1 day.

reConstruction. After Lux Guyer
House in vineyard, Küsnacht, 1929
2001–2002

reConstruction. After Frank Lloyd Wright
House Storer, Los Angeles, USA, 1923
2001–2002

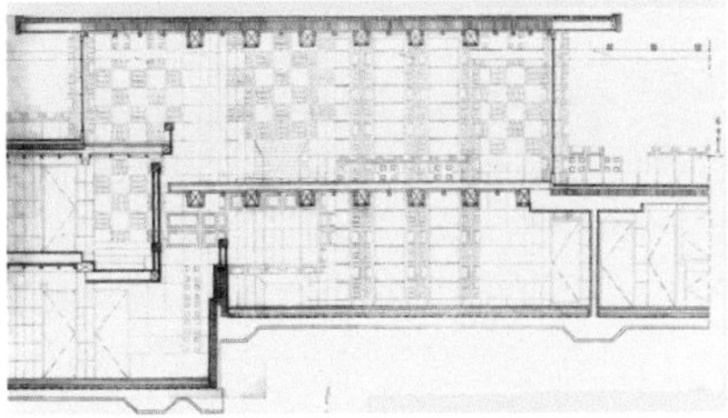

reConstruction. After Frank Lloyd Wright
House Storer, Los Angeles, USA, 1923
2001–2002

reConstruction.Synthesis

After the intensified phase of analysis, the exercise reConstruction will continue with the synthesis. For this, in the form of construction drawings and models, create a realization of the findings made in the analysis, conclusive through to the working out of detail.
The drawings should provide information about the construction and course of the constructive layers (load-bearing, insulation, and protective layers). Sought are also statements on the materiality in the space-delineating layers. Every wall, every roof, every ceiling has an outside, an inside, and an in-between. What role do the openings play? Are the windows hung outside or inside? How do they open and how is the stopper to the wall designed? Pay attention in particular to the use of materials in relation to the volumetric and spatial expression and represent them accordingly in both the ground plan and sectional view.
In order to capture the structure and building technique of your proposal as a whole, you should also build a working model. It helps you to control the load-bearing system across several spaces and stories. You will establish the themes for the subsequent models of your object, such as situation, volume, or openings, together with your assistants.
In brief, plausible proposals should be worked out for spatial, constructive, and material-specific reconstruction of the object under currently valid technical criteria, taking into consideration the maintenance of its physical appearance.
For this task, in addition to the information material from the analysis, use the basic principles in the handbook.
Submission: reworked analysis, plan drawings in pencil (sectional view, ground plan) at a scale of 1:20, models; team of 8 students, 4 days.

Constructive project.Research

The development of your project presents a process that focuses mainly on material, structure, space, site, and use.
In the first step, you will draw lots to obtain a material along with an appropriate building technique. Research your material and the building technique: What are the haptic and visual qualities of the material? How is it produced, processed, and transformed? What is the relationship of the building technique to the material qualities? What spans are possible? What dimensions are necessary? How are the connections formed? Remember to

also investigate the significance of the building technique on the horizontal plane. Basic principles for this can be found in the handbook *Constructing Architecture*, the architecture library also offers additional, in-depth literature. Look for a built reference object that is typical for your material and your building technique. Work with its plan and images of it to double check the findings of your research. Color highlight, for example, the structural elements of the building technique in the ground plan and sectional view, sketch an axonometry, and comment on material-specific detail solutions.

Constructive project.Concept

Develop a simple use scenario for a small building. Put together a space allocation program that includes at least two spaces or more, generates a volume of circa 500 cubic meters and is arranged, to the extent possible, in two or more stories. Consider any possible space hierarchies and the furnishings connected with the use scenario. Depict the spatial relations in a diagram and make a note of the approximate surface dimensions. Document the use qualitatively with a photo showing the user in each of the spatial environments. Remain open in your choice of user; he or she could easily be a somewhat unusual individual.

In the last of the three work steps, search the city of Zurich for a suitable building site for your project. In doing so, consider topography, orientation, as well as specific context. To what extent do material, use, and construction principle influence your choice of location? Document the location with an overall plan 1:2500 and a sequence of no more than five photos.

Submission: concept, use scenario, and building site; team of 2 students, 1 day.

Constructive project.Project

Using the basic principles that you have worked out over the past weeks, now is the time to develop your constructive project. Work parallel on the various themes and examine the arising interplay of material, structure, space, program, and construction site: How, for example, do the selection of material, construction technology, and spatial organization influence one another? What is the relationship of building structure and topography of the building site? Develop the volumetry of your structure. Pay attention to its relation to the context and check if your spatial program can be adequately arranged within.

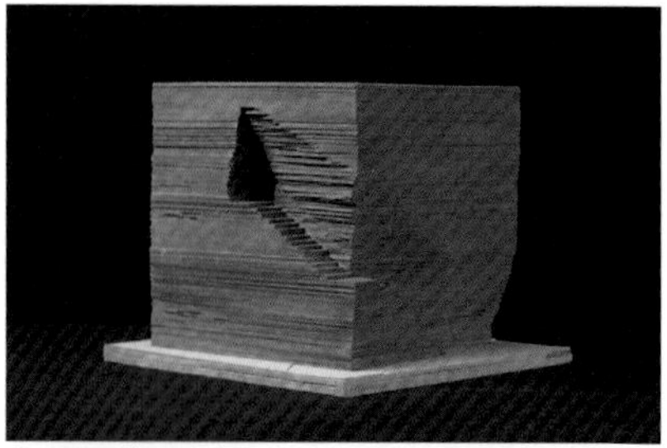

Constructive project. Matej Draslar, Mario von Rickenbach
2006–2007

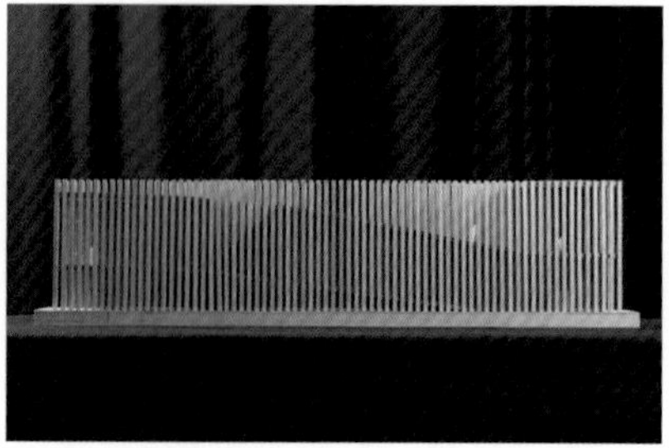

Constructive project. Anna Stoos, Dario Wohler
2006–2007

Constructive project. Anna Stoos, Dario Wohler
2006–2007

Does the building structure force the volumetry or is this determined primarily through other influences, such as use or environment? Reassess and clarify the structure in a situation model 1:200, which depicts the building site with the immediate surroundings. Build this model in such a way that you can also use it for the final submission.
At the same time, produce a working model of the building structure at a scale of 1:50 that clarifies your structural concept. Already at this stage, incorporate the dimensions dictated by material, building technique, and structure as well as any structural hierarchies. Along with the interplay of the cited factors, the main focus in the constructive project is on the interior space.
Is the inner space already generated by the building structure or are secondary elements to create space necessary? How greatly does the structure determine the incidence of light and the behavior of openings? Does the building material shape the finished surface or should a specific atmosphere be established by means of facing? Are the qualities of the interior spaces (dimensions, incidence of light, relation to exterior space, surfaces) appropriate for the use? Use sketches to investigate and explain this issue.
Depict the connections of structure, space, and opening in the form of various spatial drawings. In addition, take various interior photos (model photos) with which you can check the spatial atmosphere and document the spatial qualities.
Submission: situational model at a scale of 1:200, building structure model at a scale of 1:50, photos of the model's interior, photos of the building structure model, spatial depictions, plan drawings, references of spatial atmospheres; team of 2 students, 5 days.

Sincere thanks to the approximately 2,400 students as well as to the team of Professor Andrea Deplazes' chair.

Christoph Elsener, senior assistant, lecturer 2001–2007
Christoph Wieser, lecturer 2005
Katharina Stehrenberger, senior assistant 2005–2007

Assistants / scientific staff 1997–2007
Felix Ackerknecht, Patric Allemann, Oya Atalay Franck, Özlem Ayan, Marcel Baumgartner, Nik Biedermann, Matthias Blass, Tamara Bonzi, Sian Brehler, Gisela Brüllmann Roth, Kamenko Bucher, Ramun Capaul, Maud Châtelet, Franca Comalini, Katja Dambacher, Nicole Deiss, Alois Diethelm, Natalina Di Iorio, Christoph Elsener, Christine Enzmann, Serge Fayet Hemmi, Lukas Felder, Eva Geering, Lorenzo Giuliani, Jasmin Grego, Daniel Gut, Martina Hauser, Dominik Herzog, Christian Hönger, Simone Hübscher, Marius Hug, Pascal Hunkeler, Tibor Joanelly, Dimitri Kaden, Roger Kästle, Sergej Klammer, Raphael Kräutler, Harry-Zwi Kutner, David Leuthold, Michèle Mambourg, Urs Meister, Thomas Melliger, Maria Mohl Rodriguez, Susanne Müller, Mauro Pausa, Sascha Roesler, Martin Saarinen, Thomas Schwendener, Cordula Seger, Patrik Seiler, Tobias Siegrist, Roman Singer, Susanne Stacher, Katharina Stehrenberger, Mark van Kleef, Christoph Wieser, Barbara Wiskemann, and Raphael Zuber

Undergraduate assistants 1997–2007
Hanna Akerström, Thomas Allemann, Christof Ansorge, Bettina Baumberger, Tamara Bonzi, Michael Bösch, Martin Bucher, Andreas Buschmann, Julia Buse, Corina Cadosch, Bori Csicsely, Ueli Degen, Christoph Deiters, Angela Deuber, Martin Dubach, Christiane Felber, Adrienne Fonyo, Simon Frommenwiler, Silvan Furger, Jean-Lucien Gay, Jörg Grabfelder, Pedja Hadzimanovic, Valerie Heider, Nadja Hutter, Steffen Jürgensen, Ariane Komeda, Phillipp Lehmann, Matthias Lehner, Mikael Ljunggren, Carmelia Maissen, David Mathyl, Sebastian Müller, Lisa Nestler, Anastasia Paschon, Ana Prikic, Jonas Ringli, Elisabeth Rutz, Gian Salis, Janet Schacke, Florian Schätz, Sara Schibler, Julian Schramek, Cindy Schwenke, Eckart Schwerdtfeger, Christa Vogt, Claudia Vosti, Karen Wassung, Thomas Wirz, and Helen Wyss

Institute for the History and Theory of Architecture
Faculty of Architecture
ETH Zurich

DARCH gta

Editor:
Professor Andrea Deplazes
Chair for Architecture and Technology
Faculty of Architecture
ETH Zurich
www.deplazes.arch.ethz.ch

Concept, editorial direction, and design: Maud Châtelet, Christoph Elsener, Marcel Baumgartner
Translation from German: Lisa Rosenblatt
English editing: Marion Elmer
Printing: DZA Druckerei zu Altenburg GmbH, Germany

Cover: Alex Schaerer, Martien Schoep, 1997
We were not able to determine the authors of some of the projects. We welcome all information on any possible corrections.

ISBN 978-3-85676-278-0

Bibliographic information published by the Deutsche Nationalbibliothek
The Deutsche Nationalbibliothek lists this publication in the Deutsche Nationalbibliografie; detailed bibliographic data are available in the Internet at http://dnb.d-nb.de.